I0823244

THE ESSENCE OF

CHANEL

UNFOLDED

UNOFFICIAL & UNAUTHORIZED

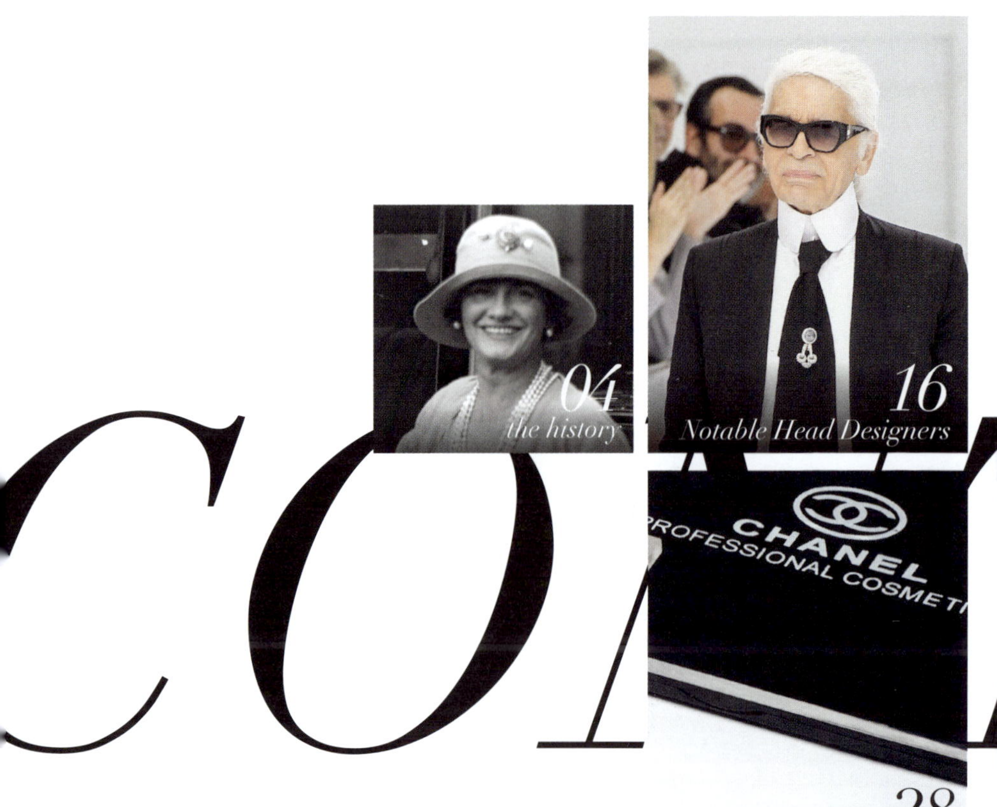

CON

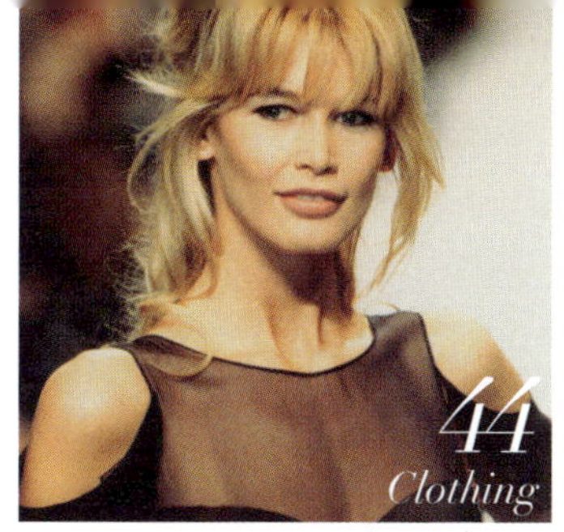

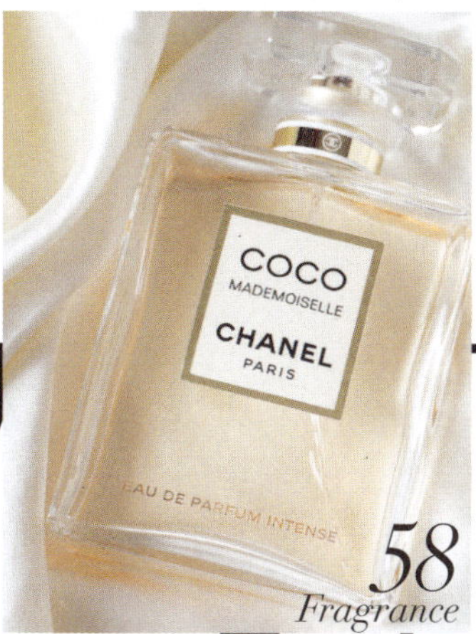

COCO
MADEMOISELLE
CHANEL
PARIS
EAU DE PARFUM INTENSE

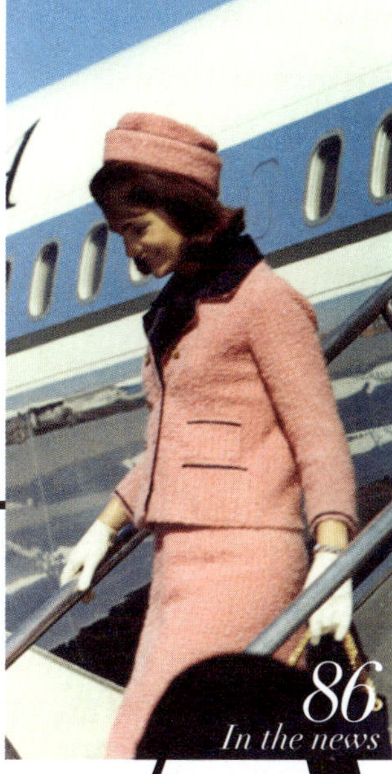

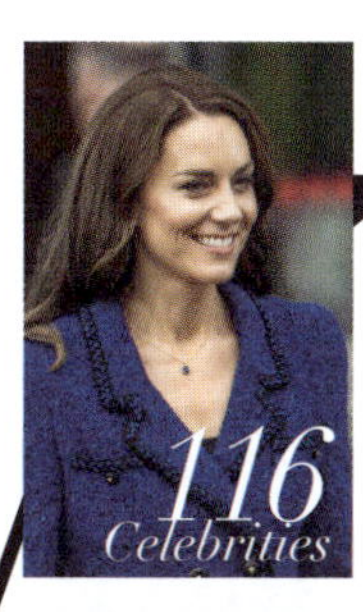

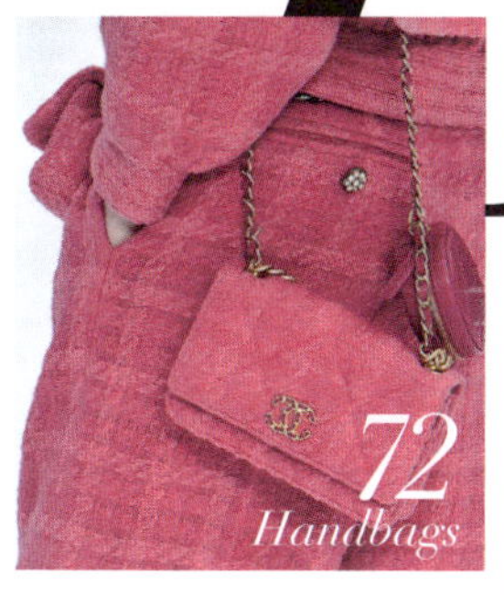

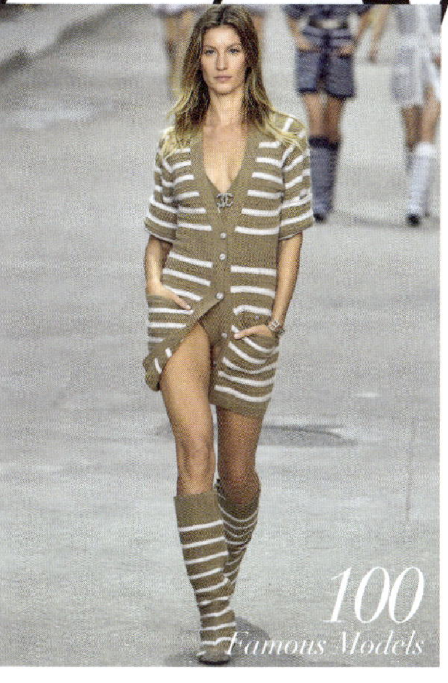

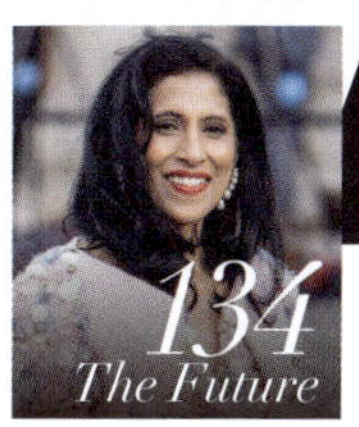

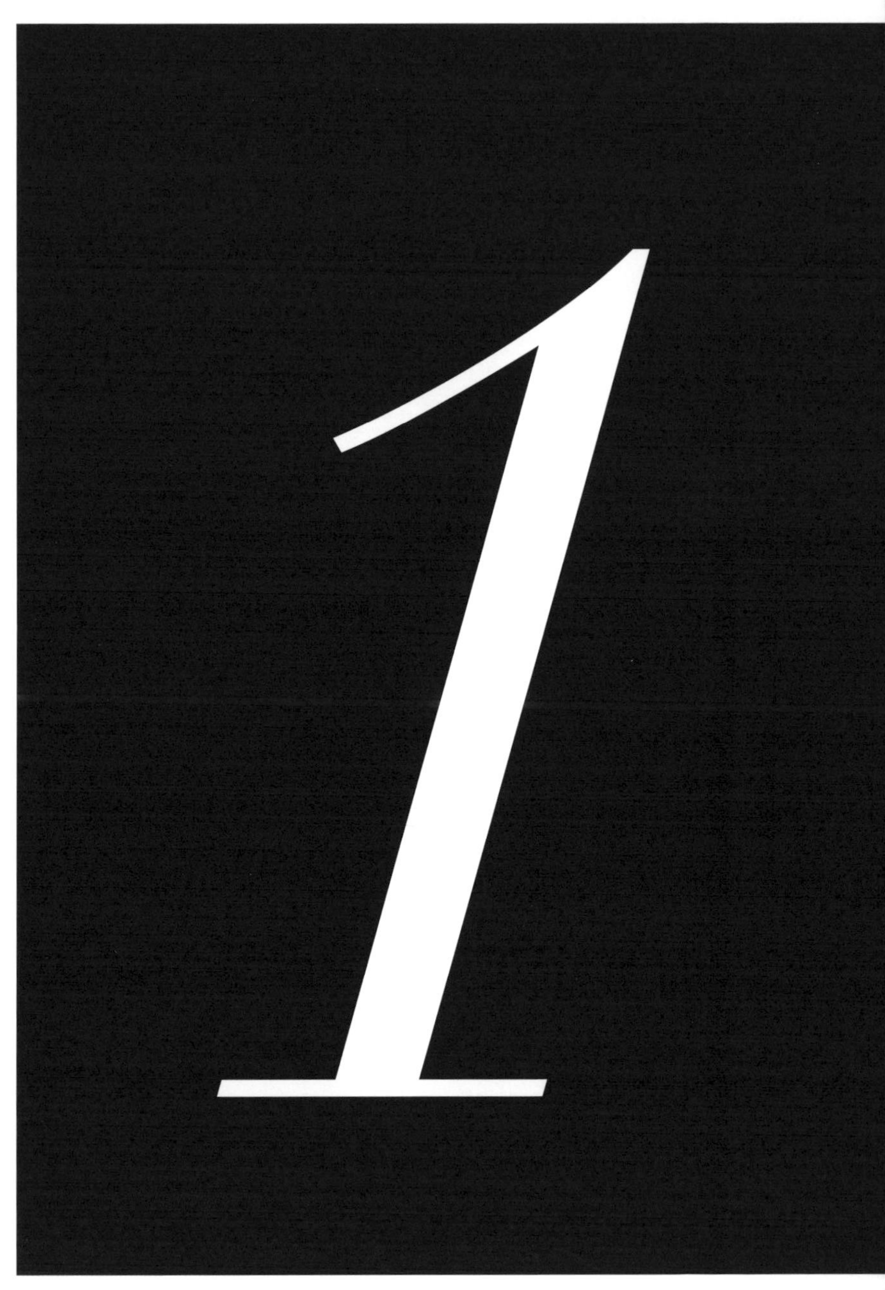

The Beginning of CHANEL

The History

THE STORY OF THE FASHION ICON COCO CHANEL is fascinating. When Coco founded her brand in 1910, it was under scandalous circumstances. To understand how the House of Chanel became the success it is today, let's first look back at the founder's life. Gabrielle Bonheur "Coco" Chanel was born in 1883 in Saumur, France. Her beginnings were modest; her parents were quite poor, and she had five brothers and sisters. Jeanne, her mother, was a cleaning lady while her father, Albert, sold work clothes on the street. They moved around often to try and make a living, a stark contrast to the life of luxury Coco would later come to lead.

Tragically, Coco's mother died when she was 11 years old. Her father was unable to care for her and her siblings, so Coco spent the rest of her childhood in an orphanage. As a young lady, she learned to sew and sang in a cabaret act. It was during this time that she got her nickname, though there is some debate about its true origin. Some say it came from her performing the song "Who Has Seen Coco," while others say she received her nickname because it was short for cocotte, which in French is slang for a "kept woman." For a while, she wanted a career on stage as a singer and actor, but her voice wasn't as strong as it needed to be, so she resigned herself to a different life when she became Étienne Balsan's mistress in 1908 at the age of 23. Étienne was a wealthy textile heir and helped her open the House of Chanel in 1910, selling hats that Coco had created on the ground floor of his apartment. Being able to make her own money independently from Étienne was fortunate for Coco, and she was able to mingle with his wealthy friends. He gifted her many beautiful items, such as jewelry, clothing, and, most notably, pearls, which would end up becoming a signature part of Chanel designs.

Étienne wasn't the only man Coco was associated with. She also became close to one of his friends at the time, Captain Arthur Edward Capel. She lived quite a scandalous life and often bragged about how these two men would compete for her attention. In 1913, she was able to open a second shop with Arthur's money in Deauville. When the theater actor Gabrielle Dorziat wore one of Coco's hats, they became a huge hit. The actor was even photographed in one of Coco's creations for a famous French magazine.

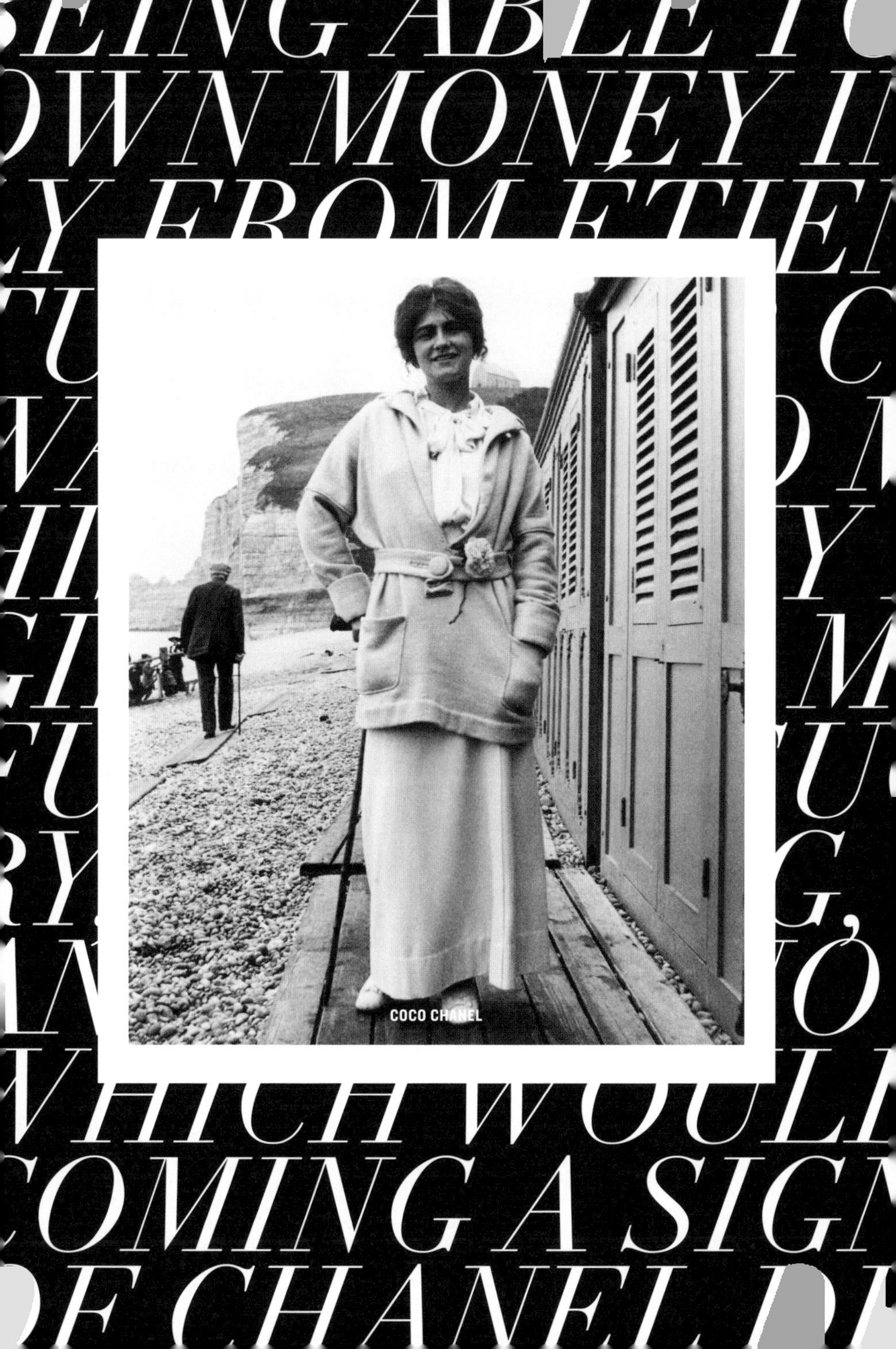

COCO CHANEL

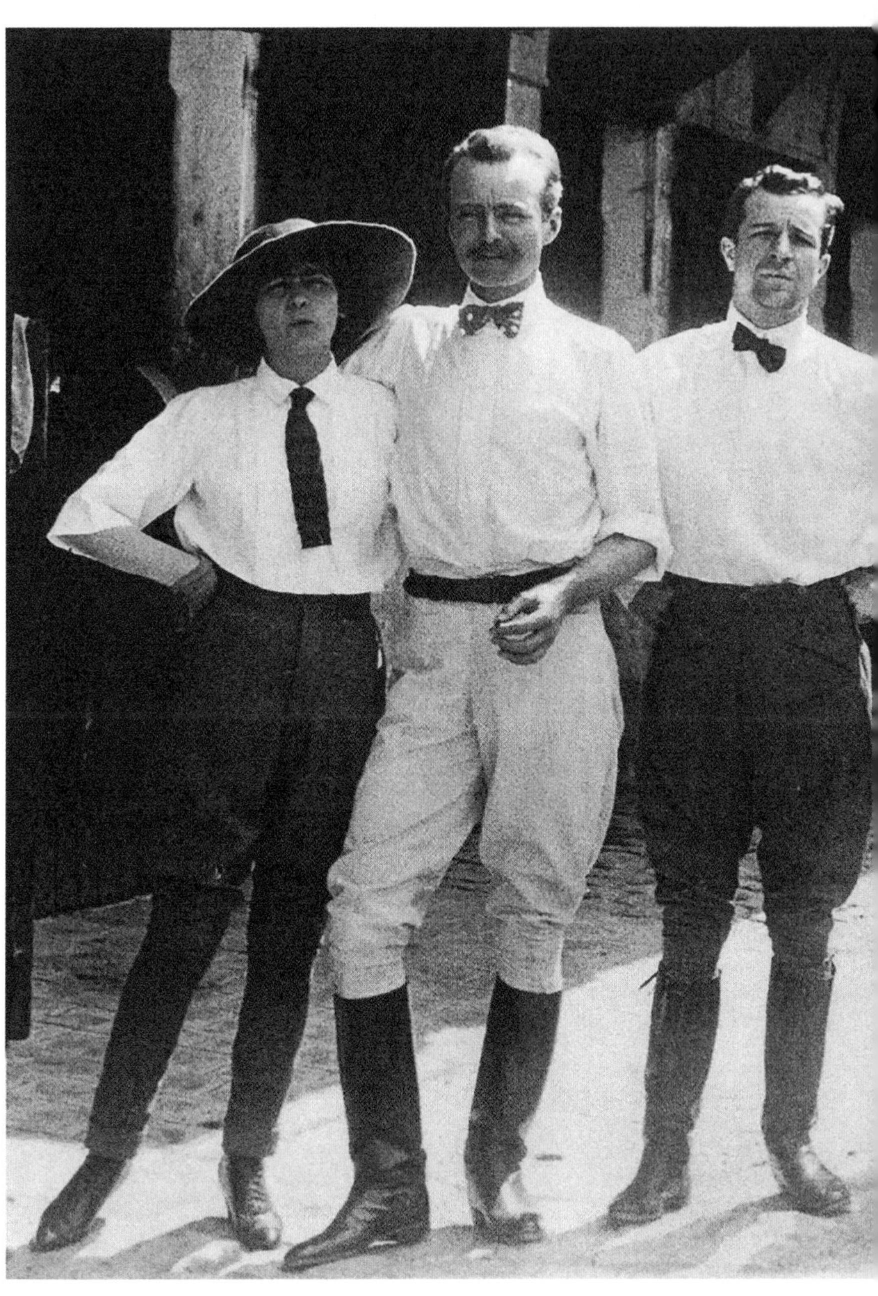

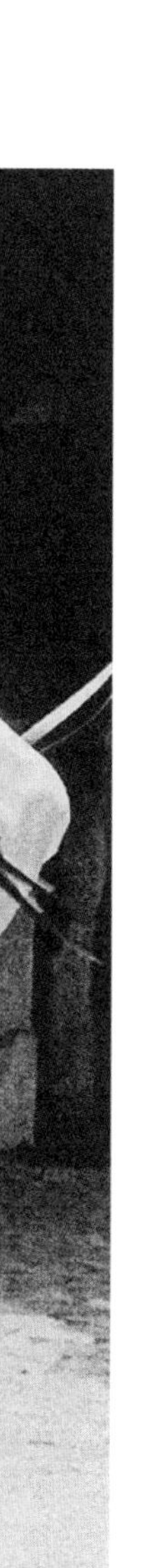

MISTRESS
Coco Chanel was the wealthy textile heir Etienne Balsan's mistress. He was extremely generous and helped Coco open the House of Chanel in 1910.

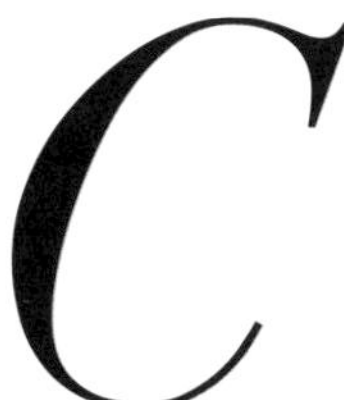

oco was able to expand her offerings to include shirts, jackets, sweaters, and a special sailor blouse, or marinière, which became one of her most famous pieces. Generally, the clothing that she offered women was practical and sporty. This was a departure from most of the clothing that women could wear at the time, so her designs were revolutionary in that way. Her couture and ready-to-wear pieces were more comfortable than the traditional corset designs of the era.

Coco opened her first official dress shop in Paris near the famous Hôtel Ritz at 31 Rue Cambon. She sold linen skirts, flannel blazers, and sweaters made of jersey fabric, which Coco liked because of how it draped across the body. She also began to put together skirt and jacket combinations, precursors for the famed "Chanel suit." By 1915, she was well known throughout France, with 300 employees and a variety of shops. Her clothing was even noticed by magazines, such as Harper's Bazaar, which said that Coco's clothing was highly sought after, noting that everyone wanted to wear her designs. Many of her pieces had jewelry and leather detailing, embroidery, and gold-toned buttons, which differed from most of the styles available at the time.

In 1921, to complement her fashion line, Coco decided to add a perfume. She collaborated with Ernest Beaux to develop a memorable fragrance, and Chanel N°5 was born. They named this magical creation N°5 since it was the fifth fragrance sample that Ernest sent to Coco. At first, she only gave the fragrance to her best clients, but it was such a hit that she started to sell it in boutiques in 1923.

Through the years and despite two world wars, Coco managed to thrive in the fashion world. She even designed clothing for Hollywood after befriending Samuel Goldwyn of MGM. He brought her to Hollywood twice a year to make costumes for the era's biggest film stars. Actor Greta Garbo was one of her best clients.

She added handbags to her line in the 1950s. Her competition at the time was Christian Dior, whose "New Look" was a sharp contrast to the gorgeous yet practical suits that Coco created. Their rivalry was legendary up until Christian's death. In 1954, the Chanel brand had to go through a bit of a revival but managed to weather the difficult times.

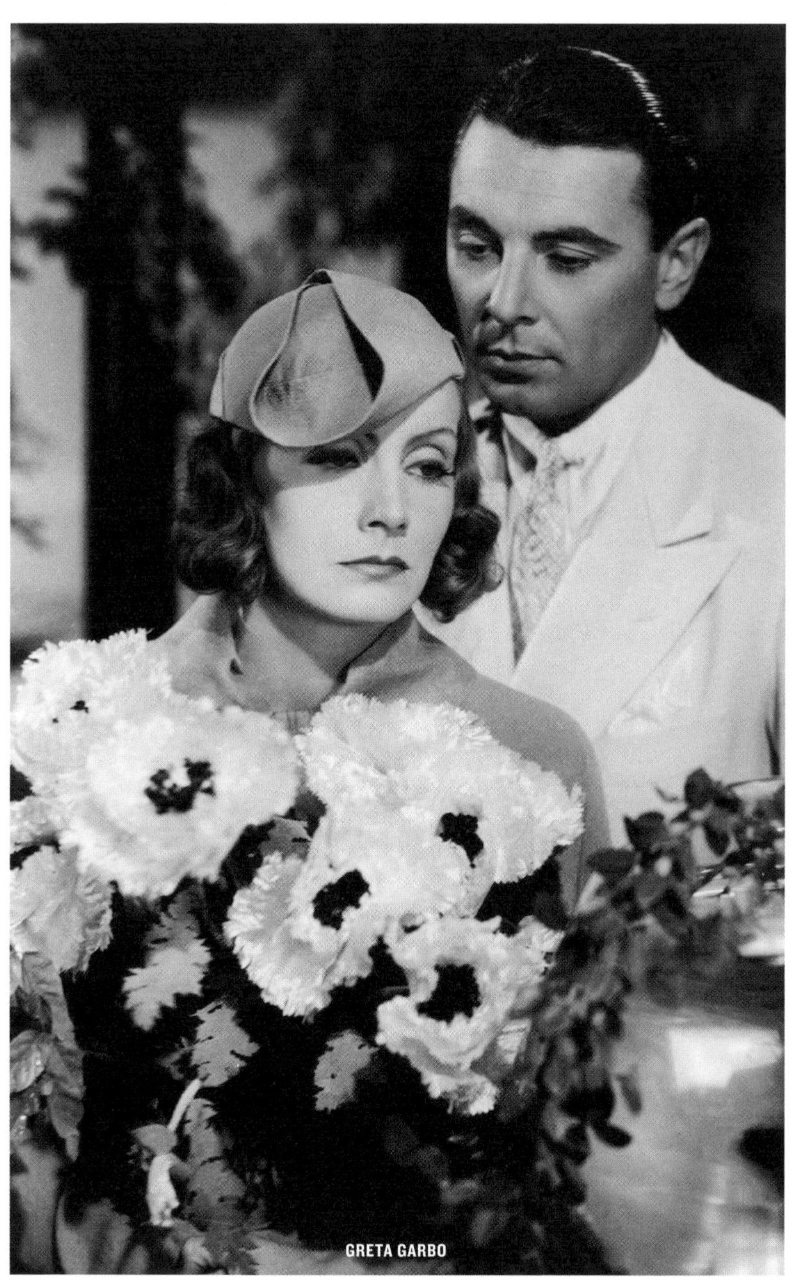
GRETA GARBO

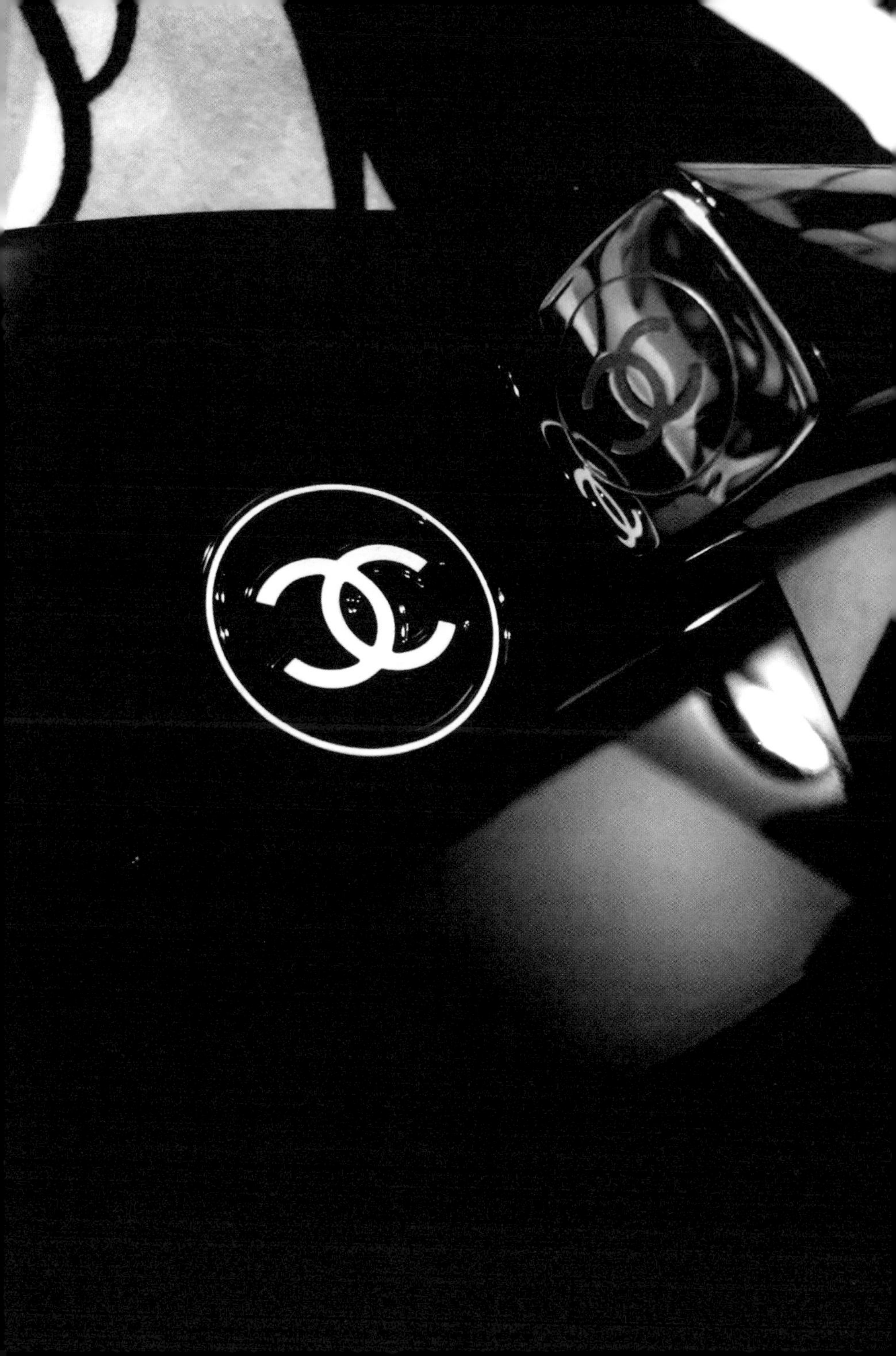

RITZ
The fashionable hotel Ritz in Paris, where Coco Chanel lived for the last 30 years of her life.

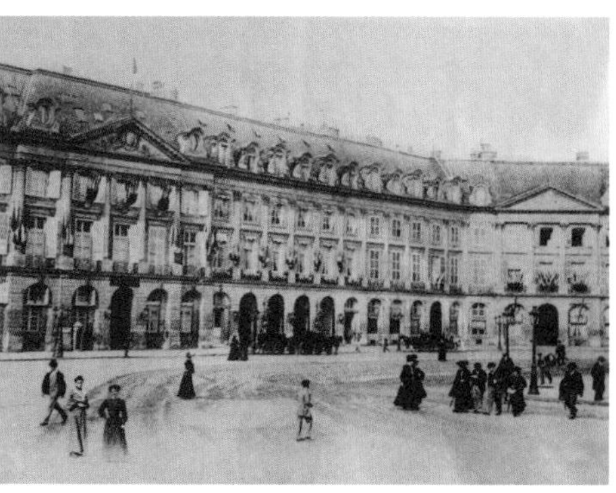

In her personal life, Coco never married. She was the partner of many successful and influential men who helped her career by financially supporting her rise to the top of the fashion world. In 1971, at the age of 87, she passed away at the Ritz Paris, where she had lived for 30 years. As she never had children, she left most of her wealth to her treasured nephew, André Palasse, and his two daughters, though there are some rumors that André was actually her son with Étienne. André passed away 10 years after Coco did.

Coco Chanel's legacy will always be at the core of the House of Chanel. Many of her designs are still used to this day, and her influence is felt in every line the brand produces. Even the Chanel logo, the two interlocking and opposite "Cs," was created by Coco. Today there are over 300 Chanel boutiques around the world with lines spanning clothing, jewelry, makeup, skincare, and luxury accessories.

“A GIRL SHOULD BE TWO THINGS: *CLASSY AND FABULOUS.*”

Coco Chanel

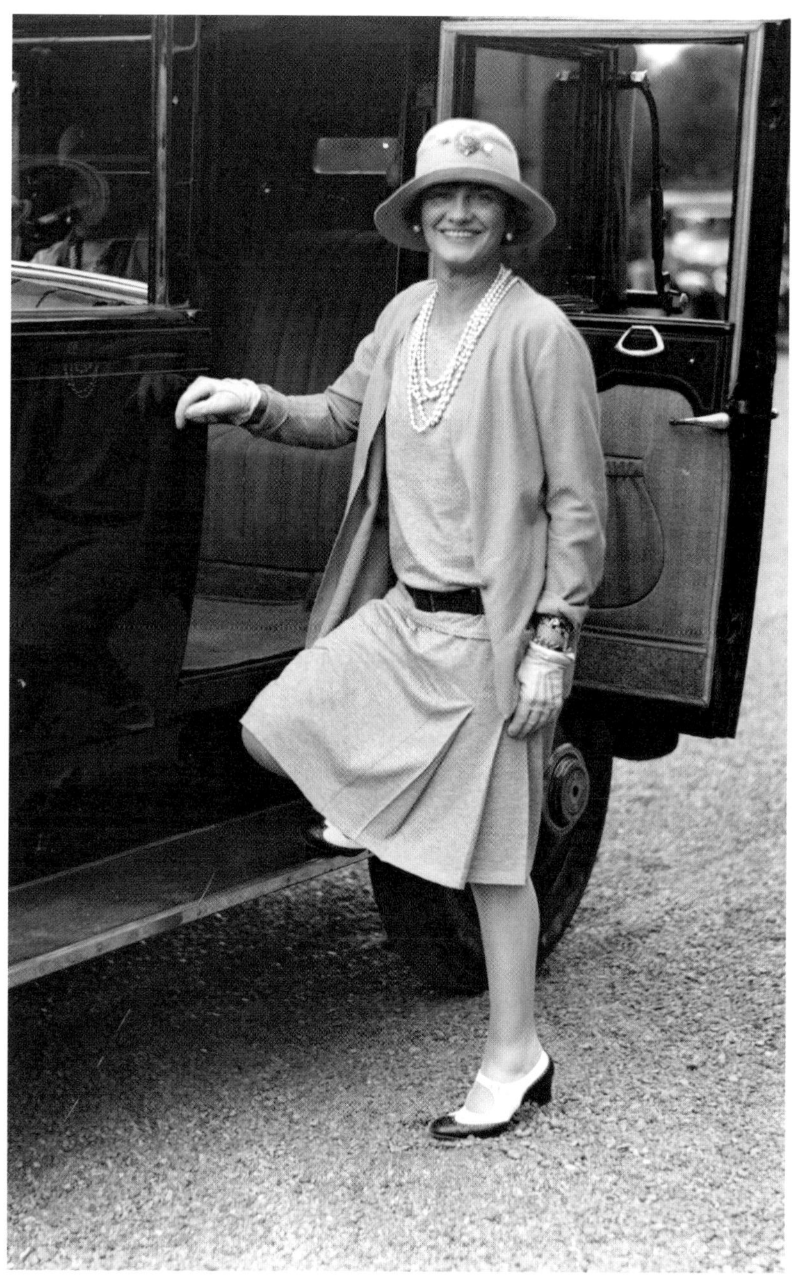

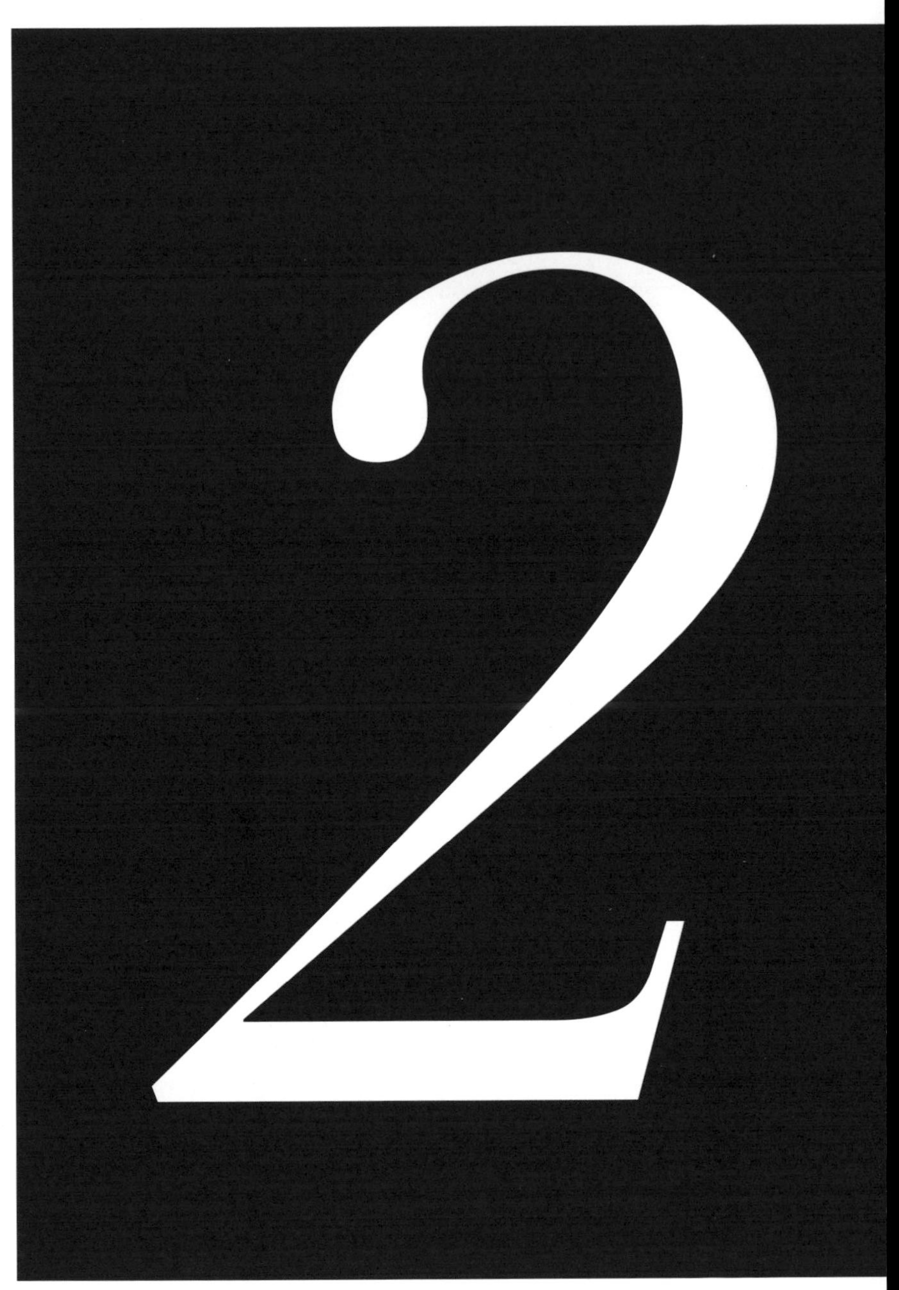

KARL LAGERFELD *and* VIRGINIE VIARD

Notable Head Designers

AS ONE OF THE MOST FAMOUS FASHION houses in the world, Chanel has a certain elegance about everything it does. The name itself conjures up feminine clothing, beautiful fragrances, and handbags named after princesses. Overall, this is a brand with a long history created by a man who didn't live long enough to see its considerable success.

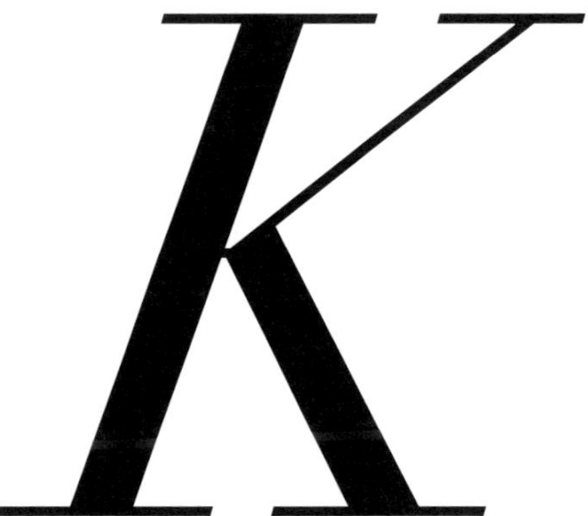

arl Lagerfeld was a legendary figure in the luxury fashion world. When he became creative director of Chanel in 1983, it was the beginning of an amazing partnership with the brand that lasted until his death in 2019. With his signature white hair, dark glasses, and dramatic suits, Karl was responsible for bringing Chanel into the modern era after a period of decline. He managed to keep the line true to the core of what Coco Chanel had created by incorporating tweed suits, gold buttons, and jewelry chains into his collections.

Karl was born to wealthy parents in Hamburg, Germany, in 1933. His father, who came from a family of winery proprietors, owned an import company. As a child, Karl was fascinated by the arts, sketching and visiting museums to pursue his love of art. His first taste of fashion came in 1954 when he submitted the winning design for a dress competition. Work with Balenciaga and Balmain soon followed for the young designer. Throughout the 1960s, Karl worked for a variety of fashion houses as a freelance designer, including Valentino and Chloé, but it wasn't until he was hired to revamp Fendi in 1965 that he received major attention for his amazing and revolutionary work.

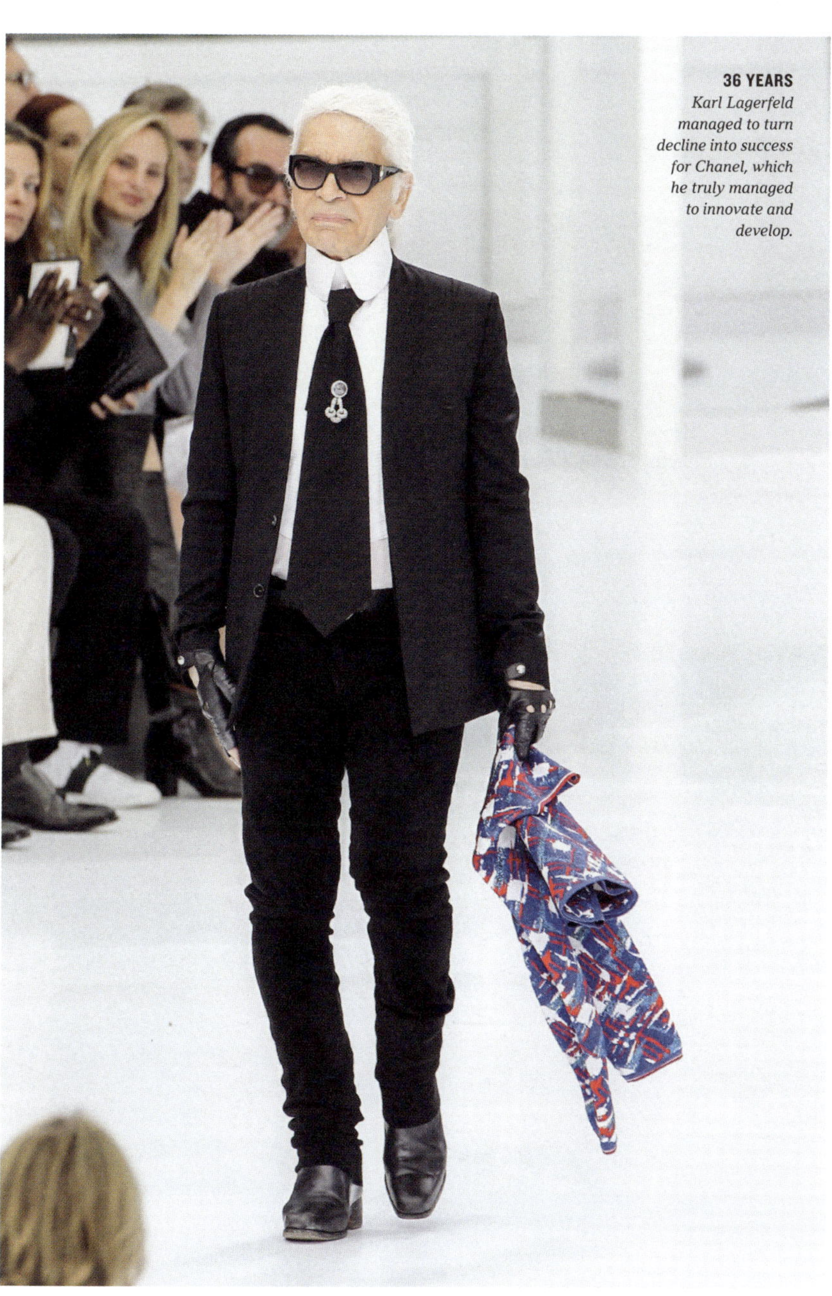

36 YEARS
Karl Lagerfeld managed to turn decline into success for Chanel, which he truly managed to innovate and develop.

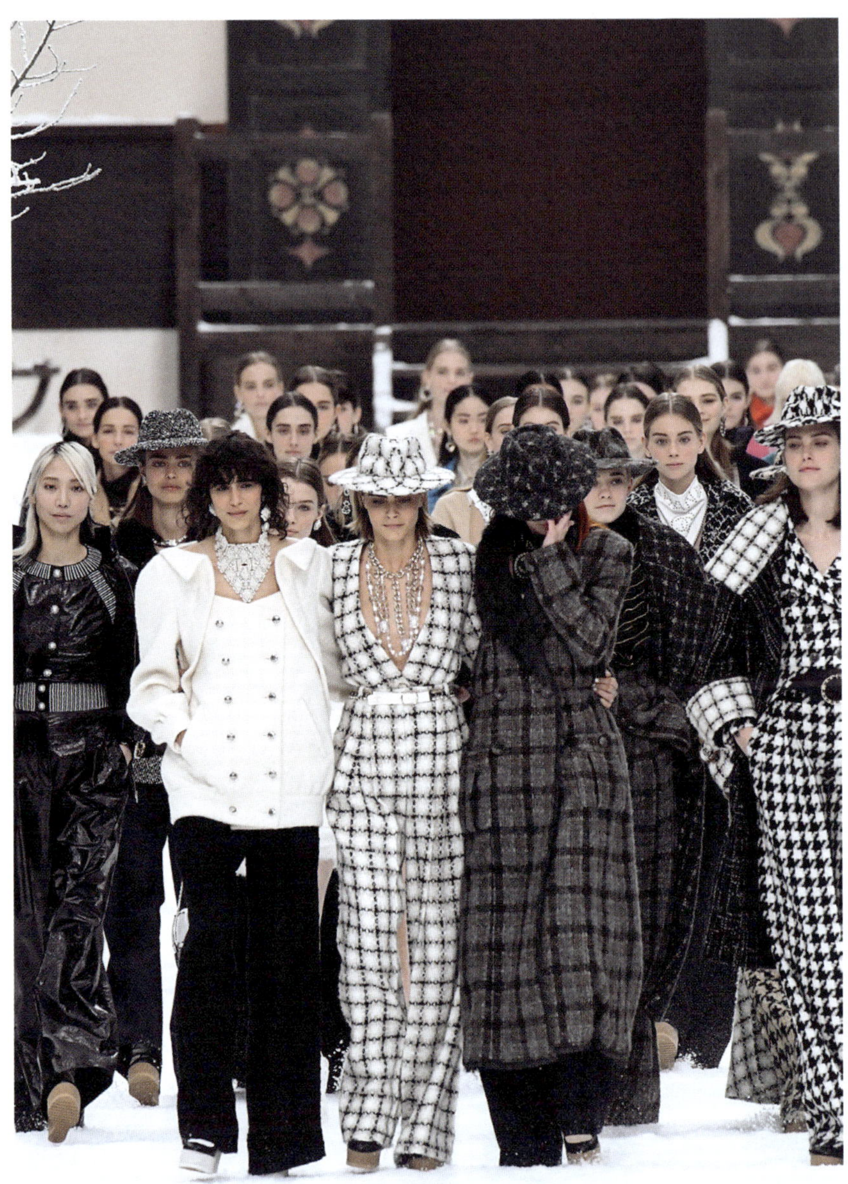

FAREWELL KARL
Tears were plentiful as Chanel bid farewell to Karl Lagerfeld after his death in 2019.

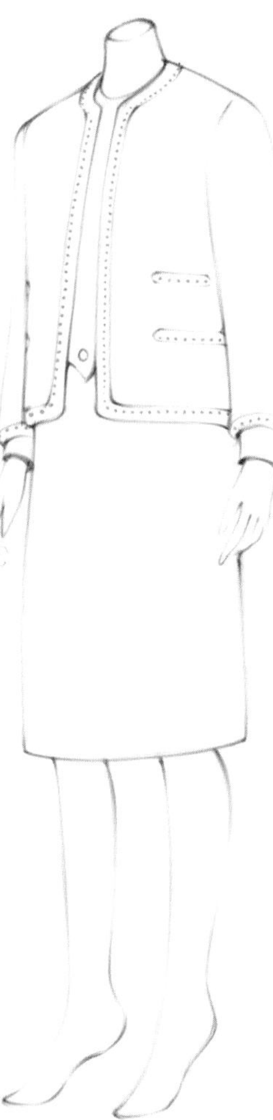

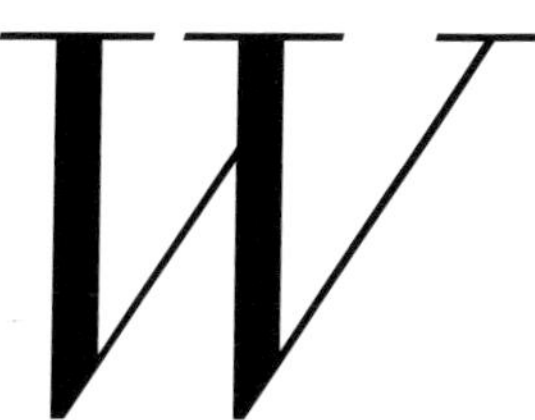

hen Chanel hired Karl in 1983, he took over the couture line, making it a huge success. It had been 10 years since Coco had died, and the fashion house needed new life infused into its designs. As a company, it was struggling and was considered a dead brand. That all changed with Karl, who made it a point of reintroducing the signature double - C logo that had been so popular when Coco was designing for the line. He also modernized the famous Chanel suit.

To keep up with 1980s trends, Karl made the skirts shorter, padded the jacket shoulders, and paired everything with higher heels. It was a sexier look for Chanel and one that fashionistas loved. While working for the fashion house, he started his own eponymous line in 1984, just a year after he started at Chanel. This line was also a success and allowed Karl to have more autonomy over his designs since he had to work within certain constraints at Chanel to maintain the brand's legacy.

Over the years, Karl managed to pursue some of his other interests, including photography, book illustration, and costume design for famous opera and ballet houses. In 2004, he even had a cookbook published that detailed his struggles with weight loss. Karl was truly a renaissance man, and as the driving force behind Chanel for over 30 years, he made quite an impression. He was a dramatic person, well loved by all his friends. His last collection for the House of Chanel was a resort ski look, which made its debut in 2019 after he passed away at age 85. The show included a moment of silence at the beginning and chairs that were printed with an image of Coco and Karl together featuring the phrase "the beat goes on."

VIRGINIE *VIARD*

Virginie Viard was given the job of creative director after Karl passed away. She wasn't new to Chanel, having worked there with Karl for his entire tenure with the brand. Thus, she was more than up to the task of carrying on the vision of Chanel. Virginie grew up in Dijon, France, and went to Le Cours Georges, a famous fashion design school in Lyon. At first, she studied film and theater costume design, but pivoted to mainstream luxury fashion when she joined Chanel in 1987 as an embroiderer. Working her way up, she assisted Karl with the ten different collections Chanel produced each year. Karl sometimes referred to her as his "right arm and left arm." Clearly, he knew how talented and essential Virginie was to the House of Chanel.

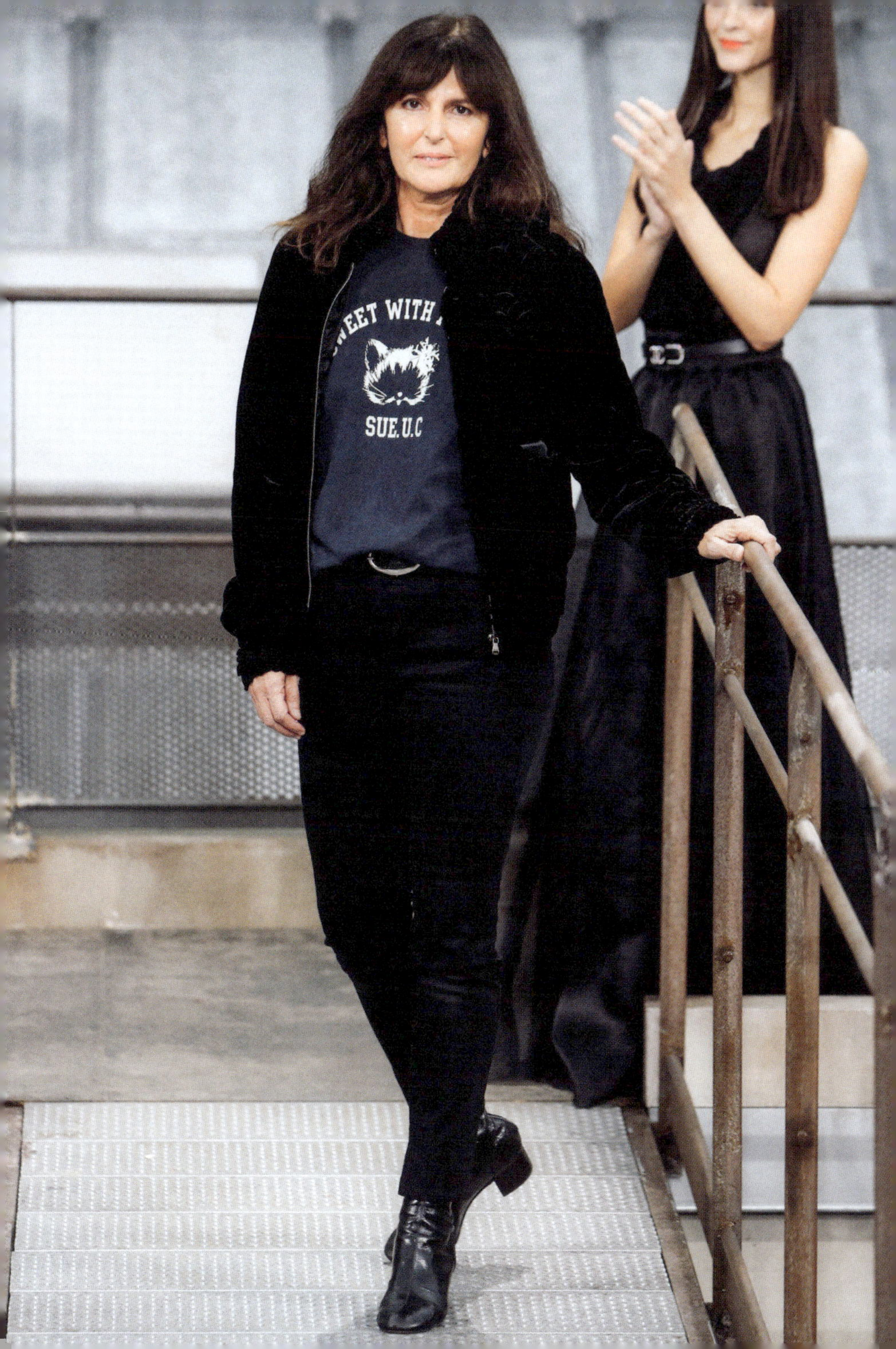
SUE.U.C

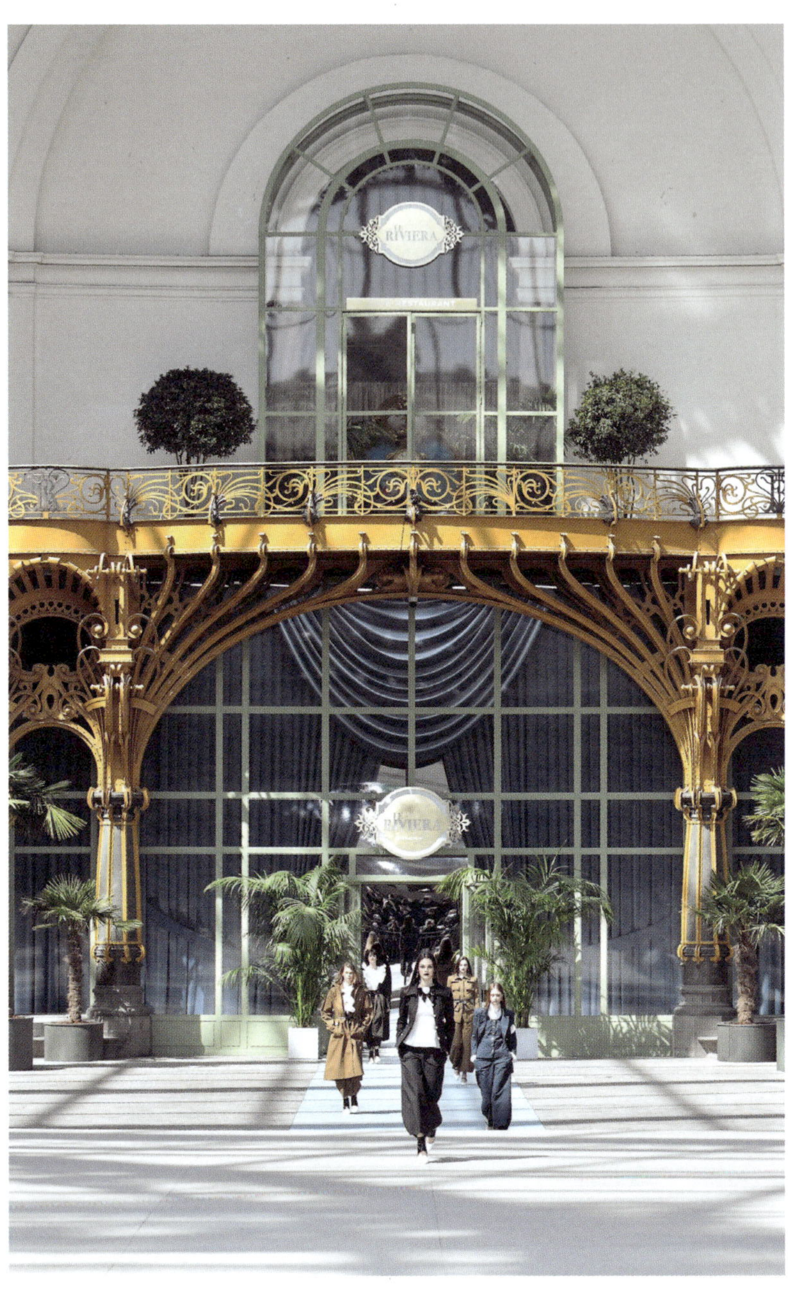
RIVIERA
RESTAURANT
RIVIERA

FIRST RUNWAY

The first runway at the helm of Chanel for Virginie Viard was Cruise 2020, where she already added her own touch to the renowned Chanel style.

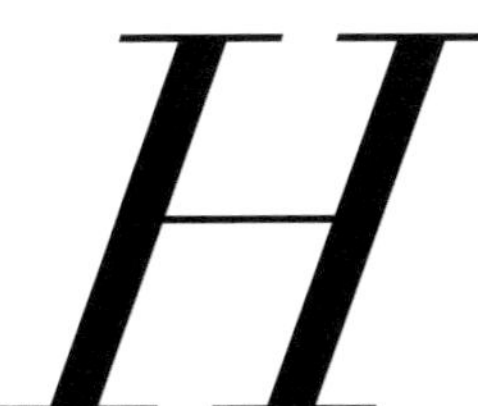

er first solo collection for Chanel was the Resort/Cruise 2020 line. Today, she helms the couture and ready-to-wear collections, as well as the accessory lines. As the first female creative director of Chanel since Coco Chanel herself, Virginie's design aesthetic is more youthful and energized. She has taken all the traditional looks that Chanel is famous for and added her own touches, including turning knee-length skirts into minis, designing variations on the famous tweed suit, and incorporating cool chain belts.

The latest collection that Virginie did for Chanel was the 2024 Métiers d'Art show in Manchester, England. Setting this show in a working-class part of England not known for fashion raised a lot of eyebrows. Luckily, her experiments with different fabrics and textures modernized the Chanel look in a way that has been very popular with Millennials and Gen Z.

Even though there have only been two notable head designers since Coco Chanel herself, it's amazing to see how the brand has changed and grown through the decades while managing to stay true to Coco's original designs and ideas. It will be interesting to see who takes over Chanel after Virginie decides to retire, whenever that might be.

"CHANEL IS THE HEIGHT OF ELEGANCE AND SOPHISTICATION."

Karl Lagerfeld

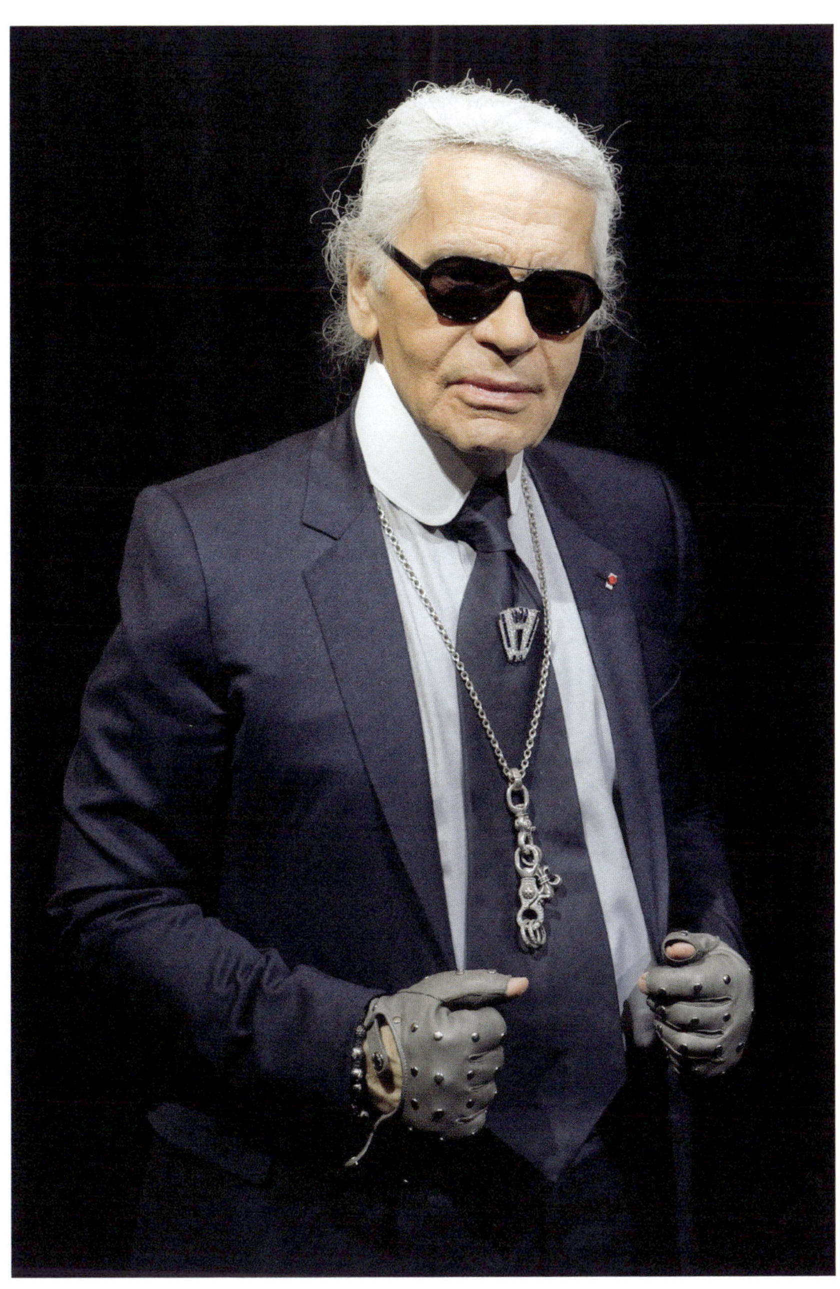

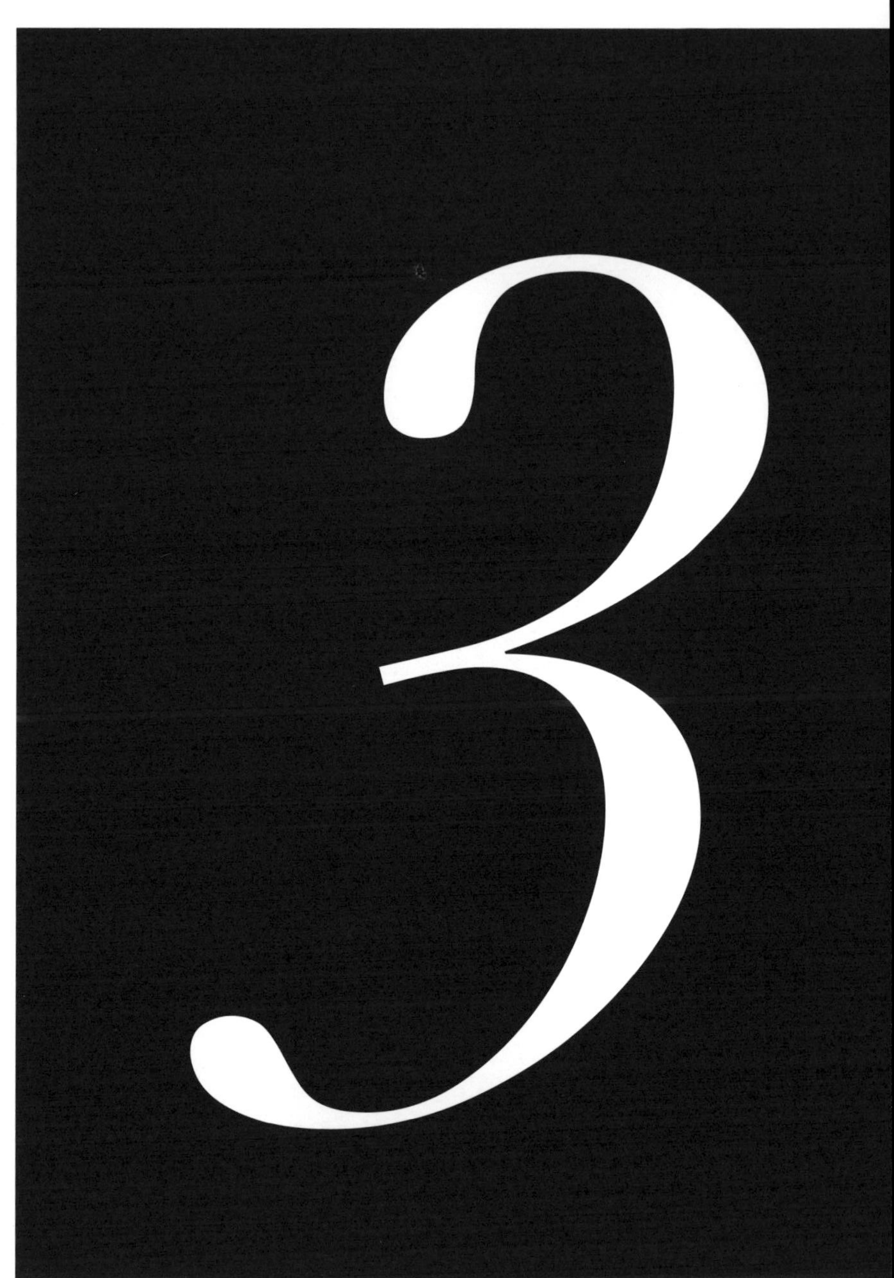

THE COSMETIC *and* SKINCARE LINE *is Peak Luxury*

Cosmetics

ANYONE WHO HAS OPENED A LITTLE BLACK LACQUERED compact of eyeshadow with the Chanel logo knows how special it is. The cosmetic and skincare lines are peak luxury and have helped shape the Chanel brand since 1924 and 1927, respectively.

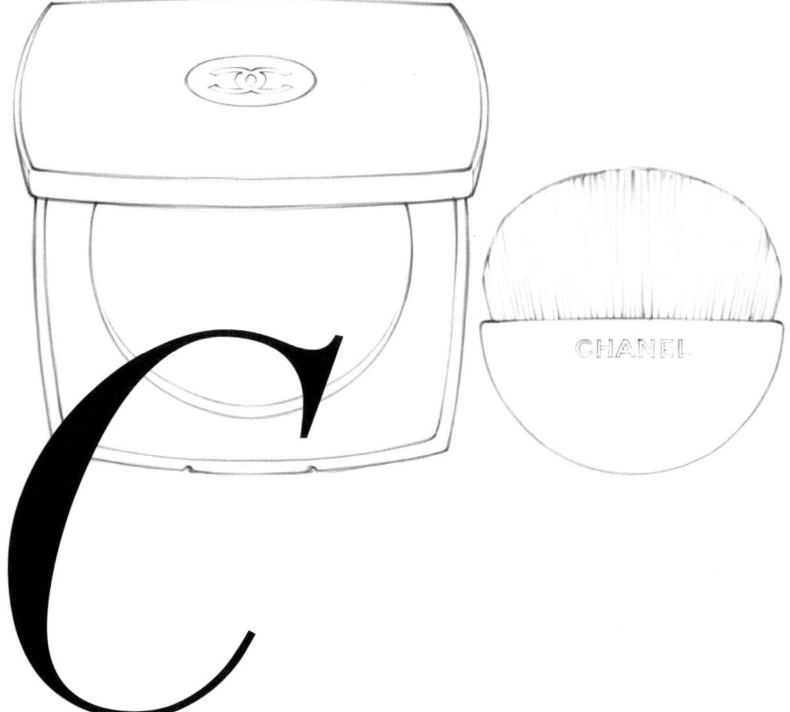

Coco Chanel thought very highly of beauty. In fact, she was once quoted saying, "If you're sad, if you are disappointed in love, put on your makeup, give yourself some beauty care, put on a lipstick, and attack." She realized the power of a great face early on. Lipstick can truly change your whole attitude with just one swipe. It's magical.

The first makeup that Coco created was a line of face powder and lipsticks. Her lipsticks were a departure from the dry, matte formulas of most lip colors in the 1920s. Her formula was creamy, had a ton of pigment for a rich color, and was comfortable to wear. Of course, the very first shade created was a red. It was Coco's favorite color to wear and very popular at the time. The original tube was ivory with black edges and stickers on each end that displayed the color. The tube's sliding mechanism was made of copper and was very innovative for the time. Today, Chanel still sells a version of that first color called "Pirate (99)." It's a classic blue-red shade, which looks gorgeous on any skin tone.

The most upscale line of lipstick they have today pays tribute to the first Chanel boutique at 31 Rue Cambon in Paris, France. It's a line of 12 shades that come in collectible square, mirrored cases in an art deco style, representing the staircase of Coco's Paris apartment and etched with the iconic Chanel logo. The shades are luminous and long wearing, with a silky texture that feels comfortable on the lips. You can even go to the Chanel makeup website and try on each shade virtually, like Rouge Beige, Rouge Roman, or Rouge Premier, a radiant red similar to the color the seamstresses of Chanel used to wear back in the early days of the line. It's history and beauty all in one quick swipe on the lips. Each tube of this lipstick costs $195.

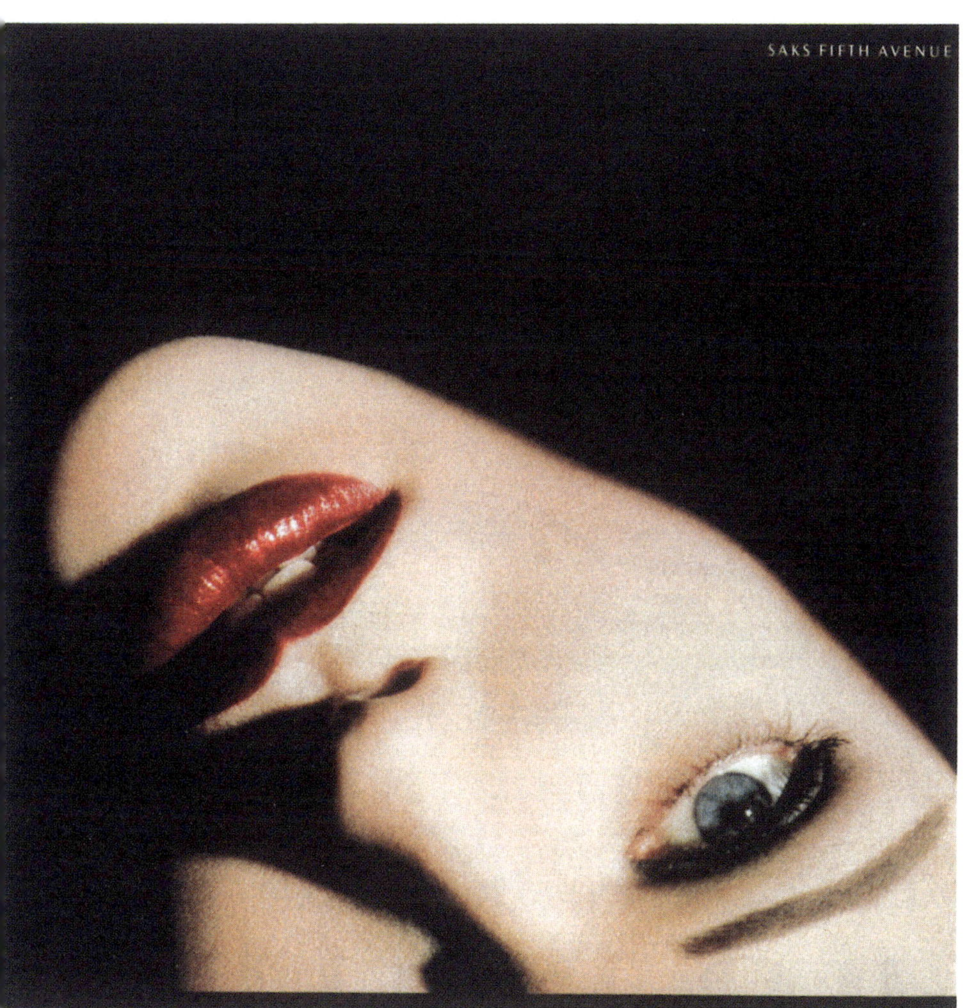

CHANEL

CHANEL LIPS SPEAK FRENCH FASHION FLUENTLY

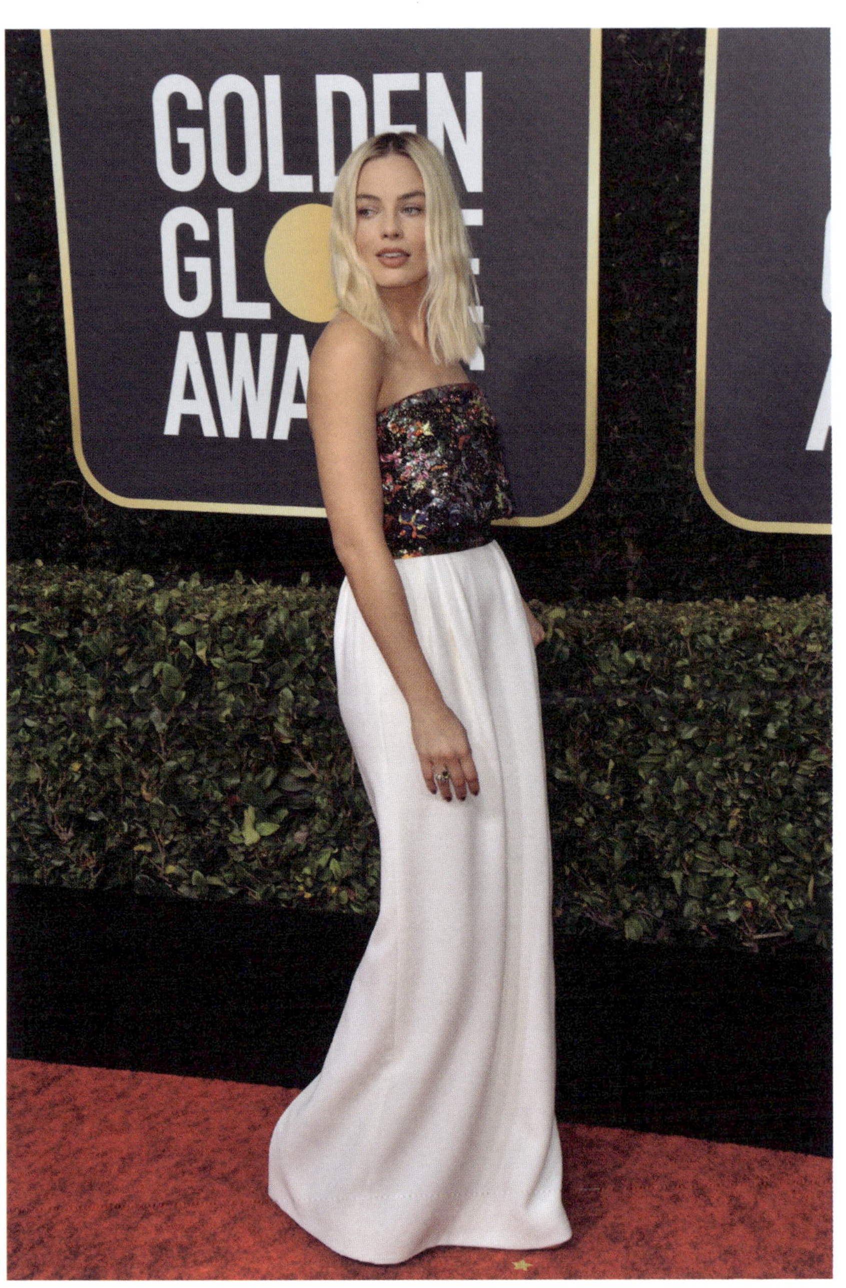
GOLDEN

BARBIE

Margot Robbie has taken Hollywood by storm in recent years. The Australian's biggest role, as Barbie in the new Barbie movie, has brought many Chanel creations to the big screen.

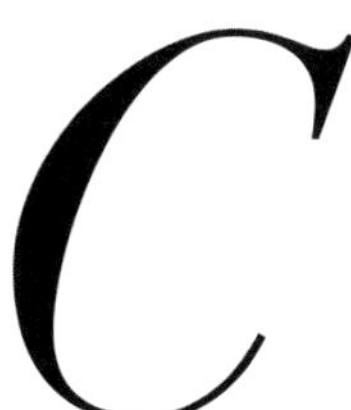

urrently, actor Margot Robbie is one of the faces of Chanel and is in all the ads for the new lipstick they are launching, Rouge Allure Velvet Nuit Blanche, which comes in eight semi-matte velvet finish shades that are soft on the lips. It's the ultimate in French girl chic.

There have been countless beauty products over the years that have made Chanel a coveted brand in any makeup collection. They are big on seasonal launches in the fall, spring, and summer, as well as during the winter holiday season. These seasonal releases are popular with makeup collectors and Chanel fans, routinely selling out quickly. The regular line is also a hit. Here are some of the most memorable beauty products that are still offered by Chanel today.

ULTRA LE TEINT
(Ultrawear All-Day Comfort Flawless Finish Foundation)

High-end foundation is one of the most important parts of Chanel's beauty line. One of the best is the long-wearing Ultra Le Teint. It comes in 35 shades to fit all different skin tones. The best part of this foundation is how natural it feels on the skin while covering up imperfections for the most flawless finish.

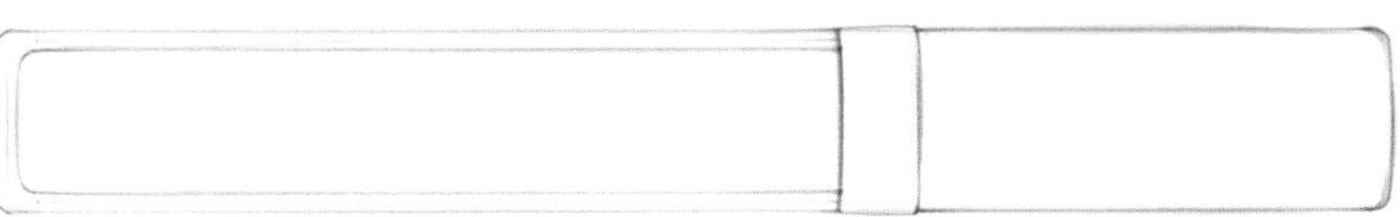

ROUGE COCO GLOSS
(Moisturizing Glossimer)

There is nothing like the perfect lip gloss, and Chanel's Rouge Coco Gloss is just that. It's not sticky, has an ideal texture, and with light-reflecting pigment in each tube, makes your lips shine like the stars. Currently, it's offered in 12 different shades, including Melted Honey, Burnt Sugar, and Amarena, a sparkling red.

LE VERNIS
(Longwear Nail Colour)

One of the most famous nail colors ever created is Vamp by Chanel. When it came out in 1994, it was an instant hit. The dark inky purple was iconic. Chanel made this popular nail color for years but discontinued it in 2015. The entire line of Le Vernis is still quite popular with new shades coming out each season. For the 2024 spring launch, there's Sundrop, a bright coral, and Lagune, a shimmery mermaid blue.

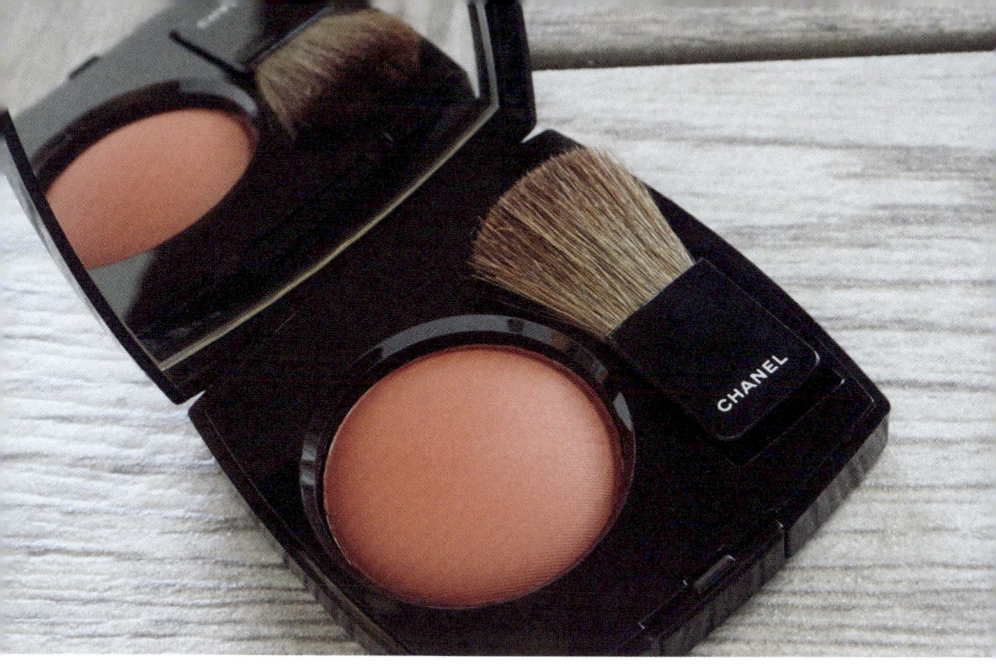

JOUES CONTRASTE
(Powder Blush)

The half-dome bubble of a Chanel blush is famous. It comes in a gorgeous sleek black compact with a tiny blush brush. The colors blend seamlessly into the skin for a natural or more noticeable flush, whichever you prefer. The silky texture of the 12 different shades means they look lovely over foundation or even worn alone for a pop of color.

DÉMAQUILLANT YEUX INTENSE
(Gentle Bi-Phase Eye Makeup Remover)

Another bestseller is Chanel's eye makeup remover. Of course, the French name, Démaquillant Yeux Intense, makes it sound especially sophisticated, and it has a formula that works well. Made with rose and cornflower water, this eye makeup remover will take off even the most stubborn waterproof mascaras.

LA MOUSSE *(Anti-Pollution Cleansing Cream-to-Foam)*

Cleansing with luxury skincare might not seem that different from using a drugstore brand, but the packaging makes it feel unique, and the product delivers advanced ingredients. The La Mousse cleanser is meant to remove all dirt, oil, debris, and makeup. Blue micro-algae is the main proprietary ingredient that helps to protect the skin against environmental damage.

LE LIFT CRÈME YEUX *(Eye Cream)*

One of the first anti-aging products that most people turn to is an eye cream. The Le Lift Crème Yeux is one that will help minimize the appearance of lines and wrinkles, reduce puffiness, and fade dark circles.

LE VOLUME *(Mascara)*

Chanel makes several different mascara formulas, but for volume, Le Volume de Chanel takes the cake. They use state-of-the-art technology to achieve instant volume, texture, and length for the most glamorous lashes possible. You can buy it for $40 a pop in black, brown, or navy.

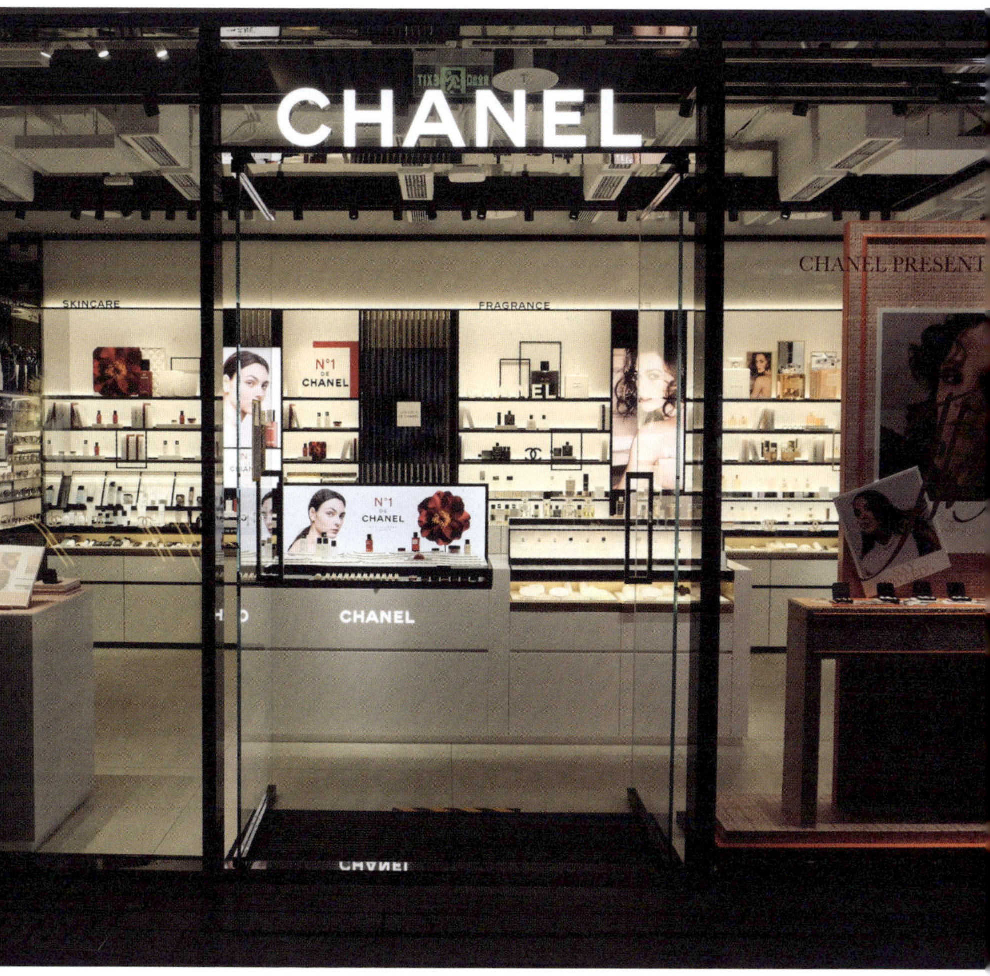

N°1 DE CHANEL REVITALIZING SERUM

One of Chanel's newest skincare products is the N°1 de Chanel Revitalizing Serum. It's part of a newer holistic approach to skincare and features red camellia extract. The goal is to prevent and correct the five main signs of aging, and it works for all skin types, including sensitive skin. Plus, it feels silky and luxurious underneath makeup.

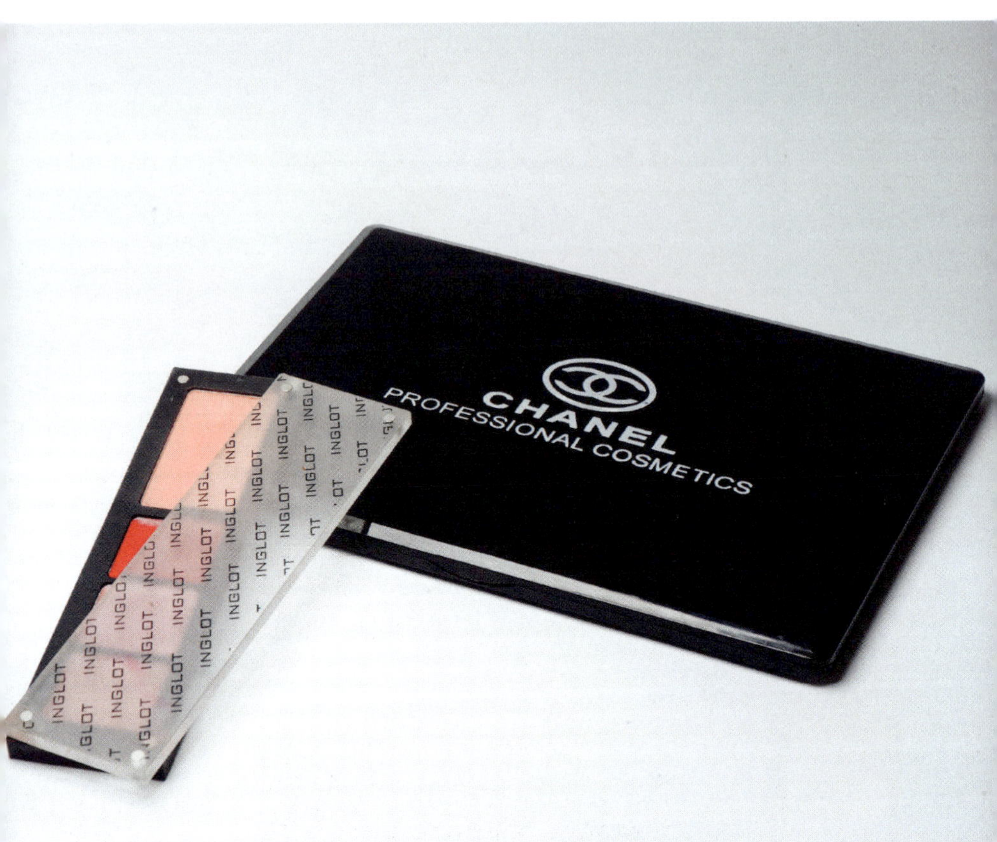

LES 4 OMBRES *(Multi-Effect Quadra Eyeshadow)*

Another excellent product that Chanel makes is eyeshadow. Les 4 Ombres is a four-pack of highly pigmented, long-wearing eyeshadows that come in a multitude of colors to choose from. The fun thing about these eyeshadows is that they do seasonal releases, which come in all types of colors and patterns. Sometimes the Chanel tweed texture is imprinted on the eyeshadows, while other times floral patterns or other prints are embossed on them. They are a work of art in and of themselves and almost too pretty to use.

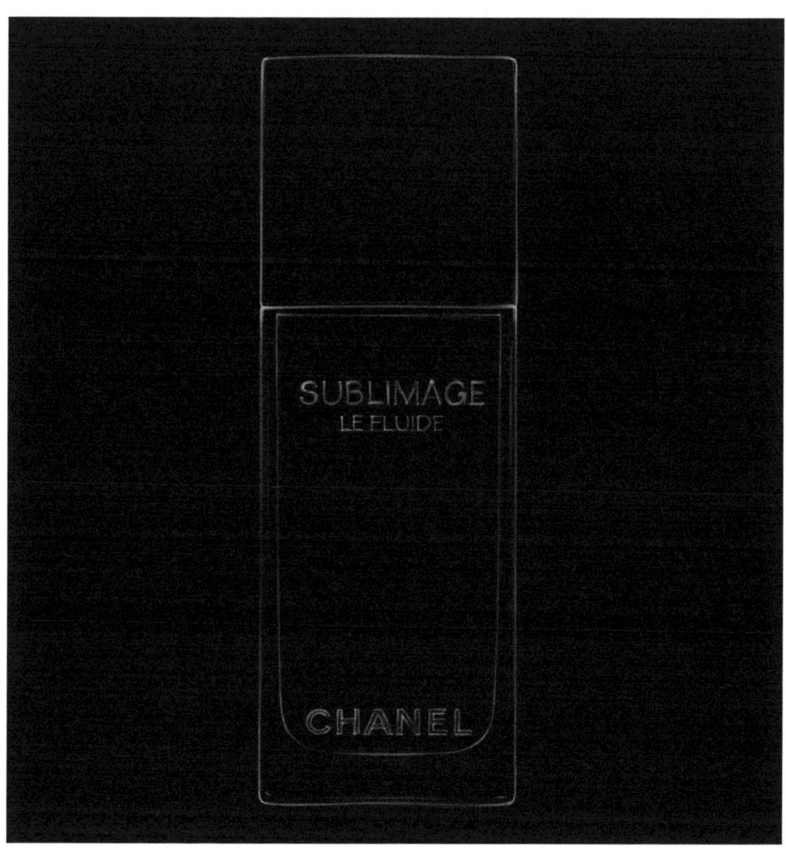

THE SKINCARE

The skincare line started out with just 12 products. Today, it spans hundreds, including the best-selling lines Sublimage, Le Lift, Le Lift Pro, and Hydra Beauty. Here are a few of the top-notch products in Chanel's luxury skincare line.

"I LOVE CHANEL MAKEUP. *I FEEL LIKE IT'S VERY CHIC. YOU CAN DO A LOT WITH JUST A LITTLE BIT.* IT'S CLASSIC"

Kristen Stewart

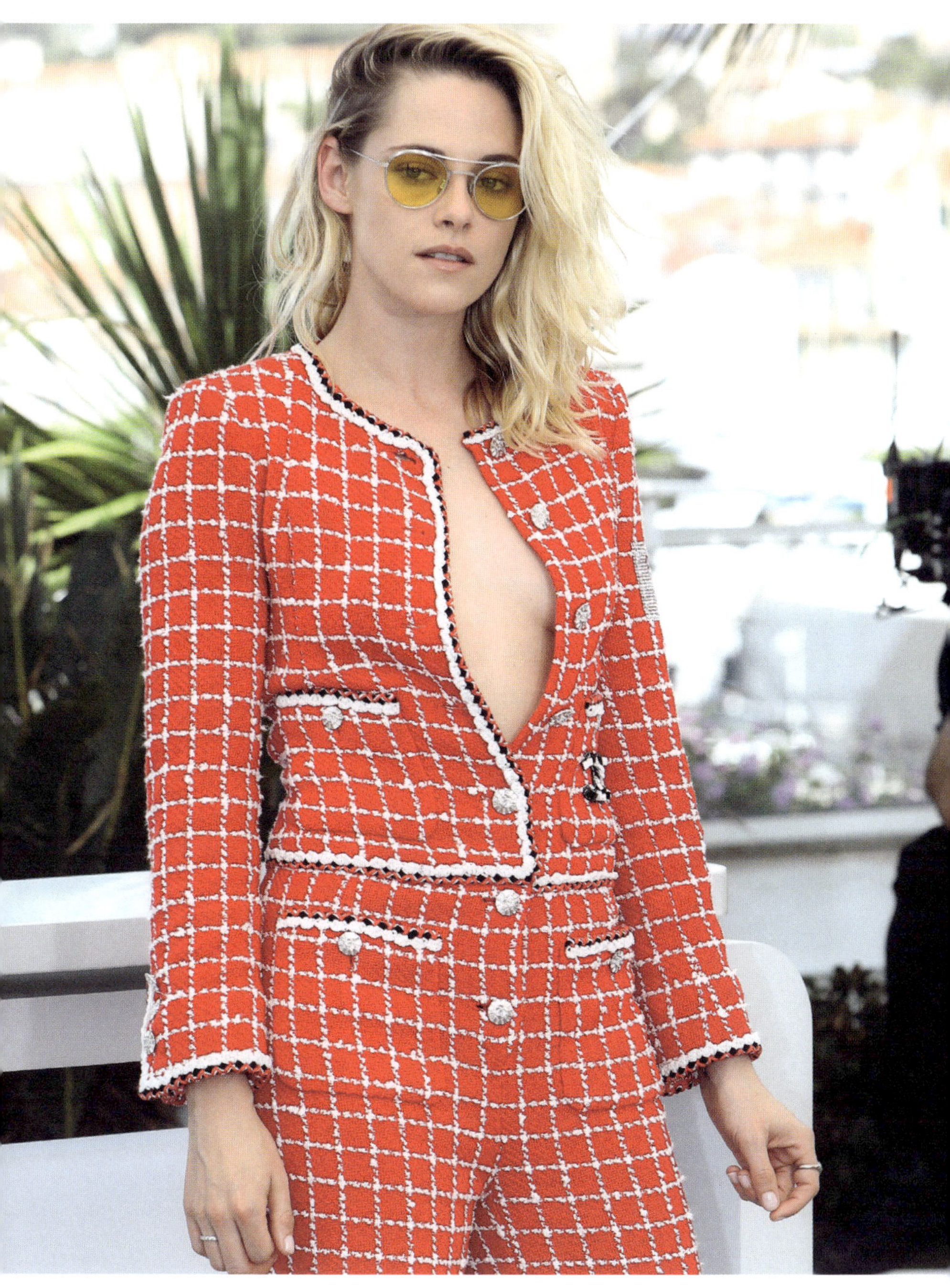

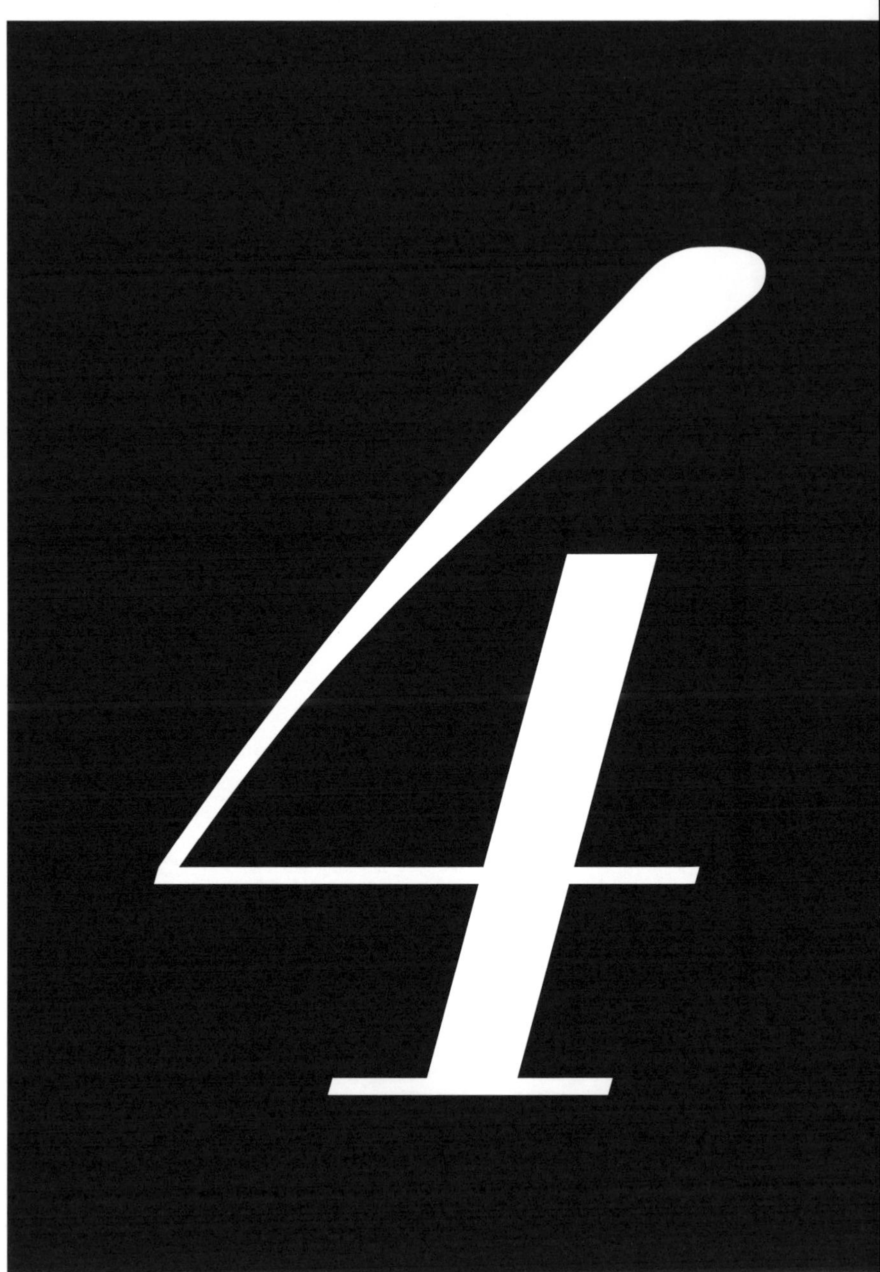

THE ICONIC CHANEL TWEED SUIT *and* BEYOND

Clothing

WHEN YOU PICTURE CHANEL CLOTHING, the first thing that likely comes to mind is the classic tweed suit. This suit, which Coco Chanel created back in the 1920s, was quite a departure from much of the clothing available for women at the time. She chose tweed for the material since it was more durable and longer lasting than other fabrics. The silhouette of the suit was also entirely different from that of the popular styles from other designers, such as Christian Dior, which featured tight corsets and cinched waists. They had a famed rivalry, and Coco was more than happy to compete with Mr. Dior.

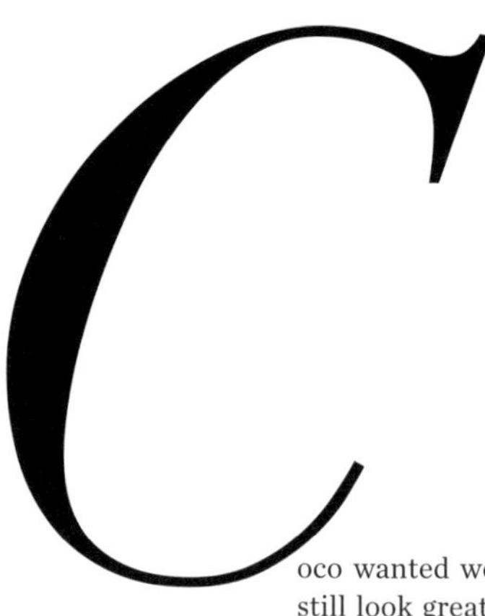

oco wanted women to be able to move, be comfortable, and still look great in their clothing. The boxy Chanel tweed suit was characterized by a collarless jacket, slim-fitting skirt, and gold buttons on the top, which would become a signature look of the brand. The design was meant to be both feminine and empowering because women could actually do things in Coco's tweed suits.

The Chanel tweed suit has been worn by many famous women over the years, including Princess Diana, Jackie Kennedy, Brigitte Bardot, and Barbara Walters. To own a Chanel suit is to own a piece of history, one that has been reinterpreted for each new style era.

When Karl Lagerfeld joined the House of Chanel as creative director in 1983, he made subtle changes to the classic Chanel suit. He made these changes gradually because while he wanted to make the Chanel suit his own as a designer, he didn't want to insult the memory of Coco, who had created such a masterpiece for the design house. Some of the collections he did featured the suit in new materials, such as denim and bright neon wool, and he even created a tweed bralette to go with the suit. During the 1990s, he especially liked to challenge the aesthetic of Chanel, making it sexier to go with the hottest supermodels of the decade who walked the runway, including Linda Evangelista, Christy Turlington, and Helena Christenson. For example, Helena wore a version of the Chanel tweed suit with a mesh shirt underneath, which was completely see-through, with ropes of Chanel gold chains. It was an incredibly sexy and memorable look for the line.

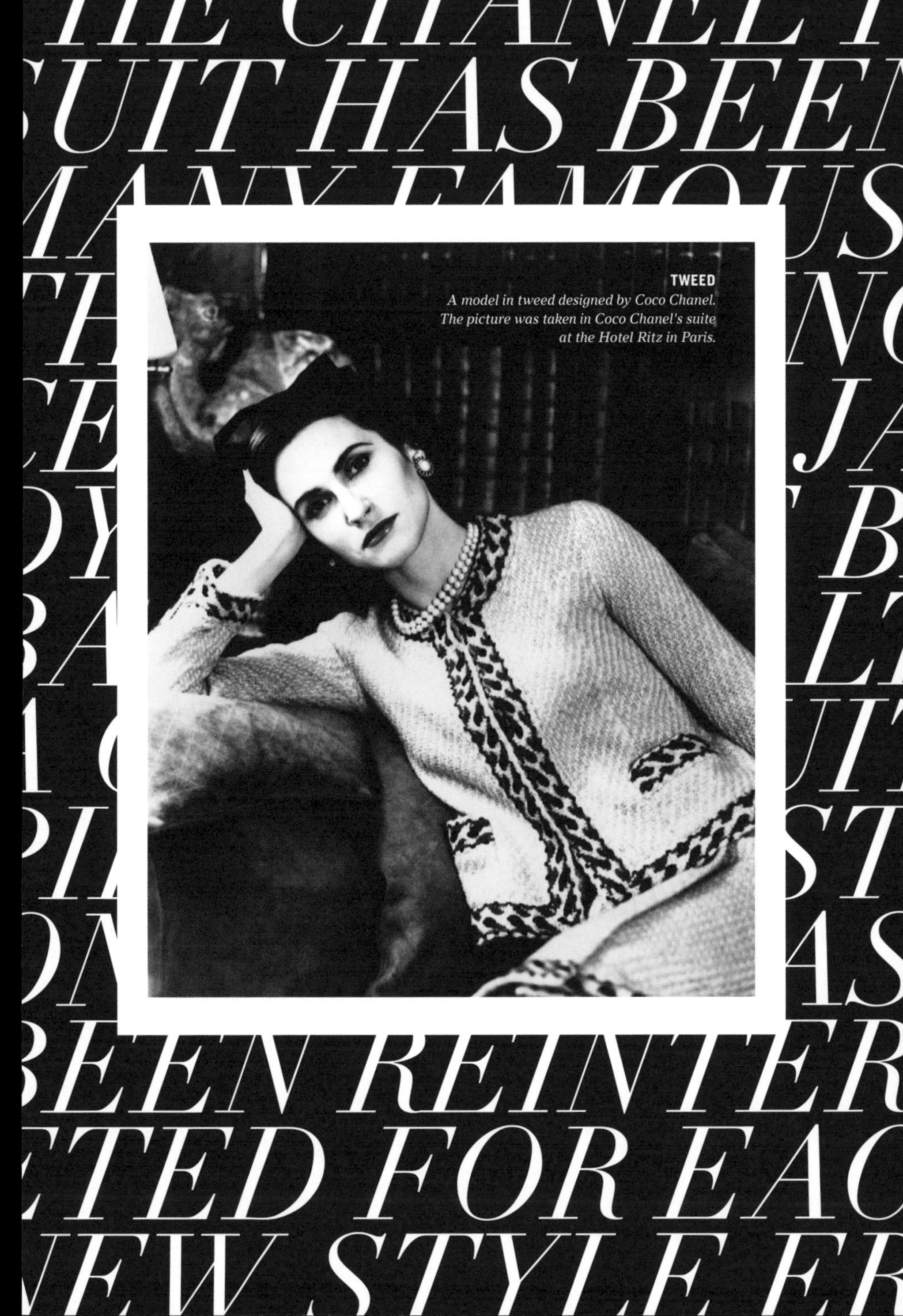

TWEED
A model in tweed designed by Coco Chanel. The picture was taken in Coco Chanel's suite at the Hotel Ritz in Paris.

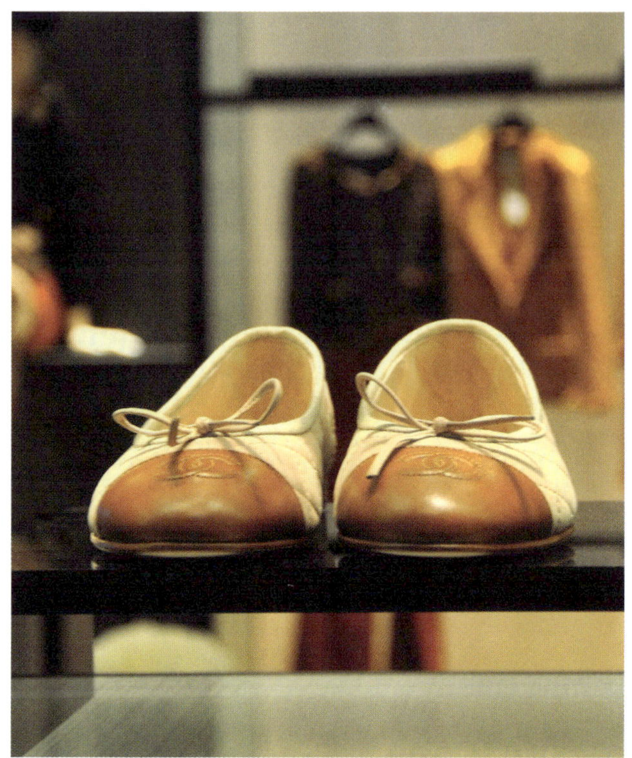

THE CHANEL *Ballet Flat*

Chanel isn't only famous for its tweed suits. There have been many other styles and pieces over the years that have been a hit for the House of Chanel. One of their most famous items, a classic that many women have owned, is the Chanel ballet shoe. The signature ballet flat is a beauty with the Chanel logo stitched on top, a ribbon accent, and a hint of heel. They are comfortable and easy to travel with. The best part is that they go with so many different looks, from jeans to skirts and everything in between. This amazing shoe made its debut in the Spring/Summer 1984 collection and has been popular ever since. Here are some other collections that have been important parts of Chanel's history.

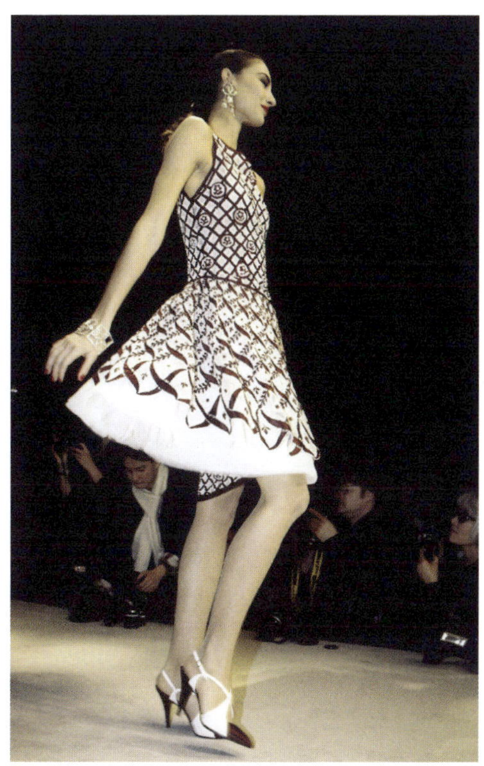

SPRING/SUMMER *1987*

The gorgeous sequined dresses on the runway for this show were designed by Karl for the haute couture collection. Sleeveless, with bows on the front, and in basic colors like black and white, each dress was both classic and unique. In addition, there was a diagonally cut Chanel suit, pants with bolero jackets, and high-waisted skirts. It was a departure from the usual and received some criticism at the time, but overall people loved the looks on models such as Naomi Campbell and Linda Evangelista. The show was held at the École Nationale Supérieure des Beaux-Arts in Paris.

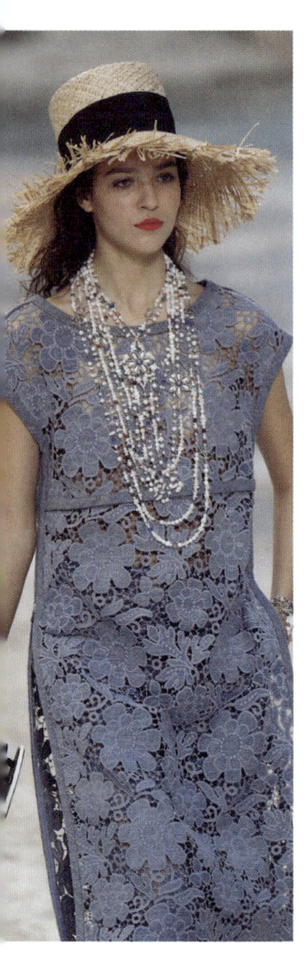

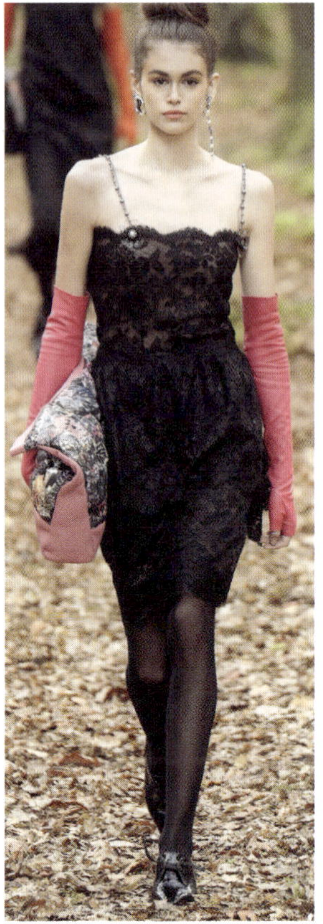

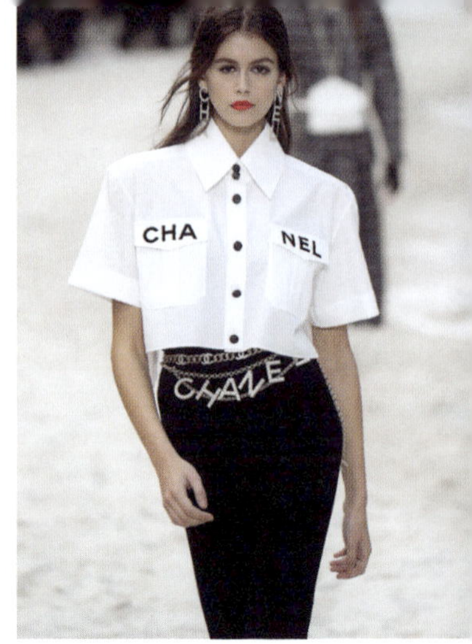
CHA
NEL

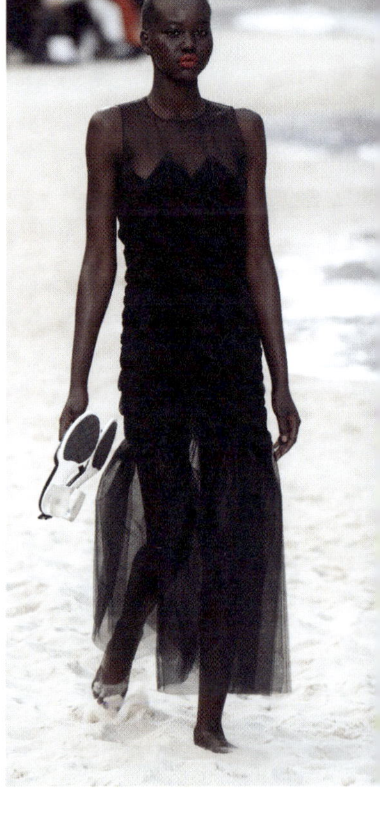

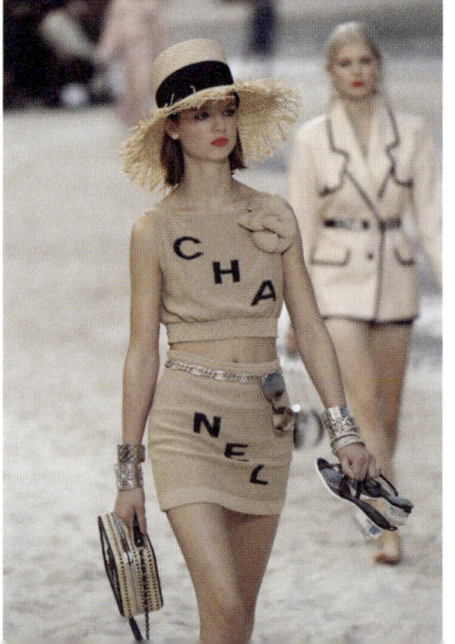
CHA
NEL

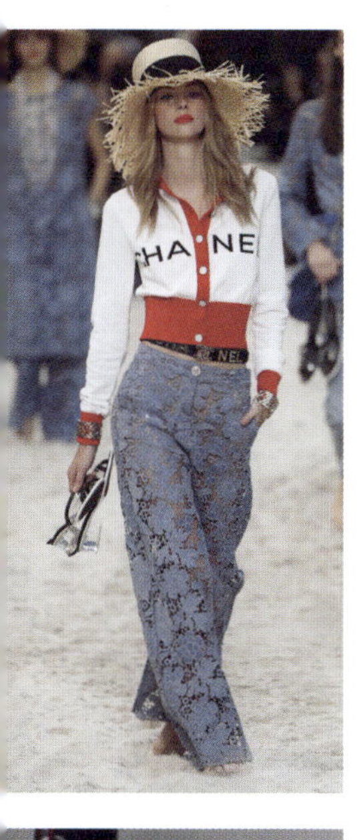

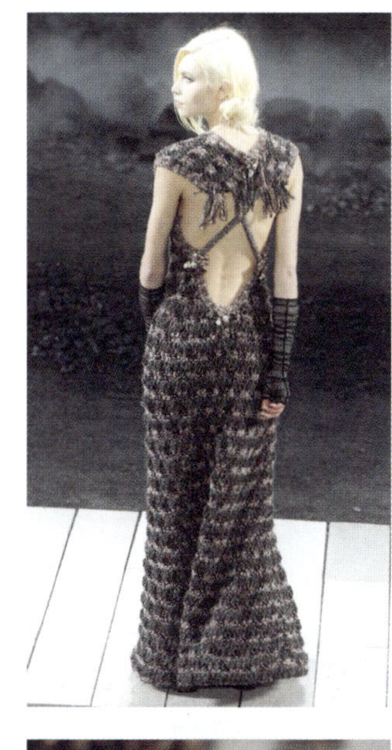

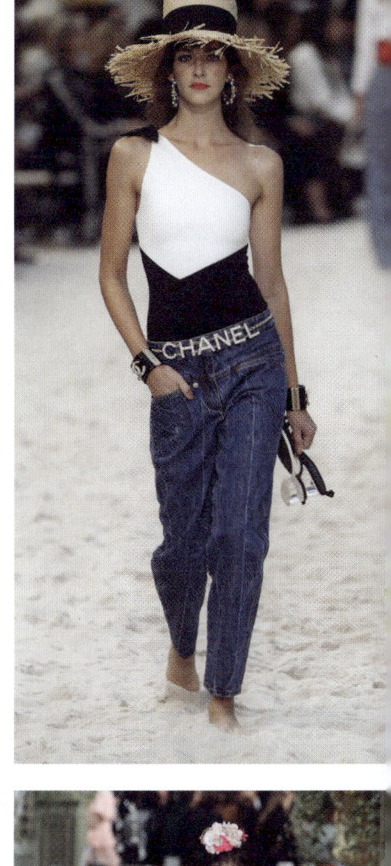
CHANEL

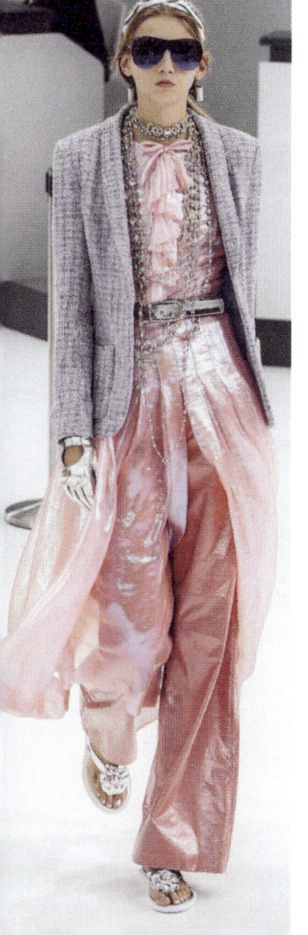

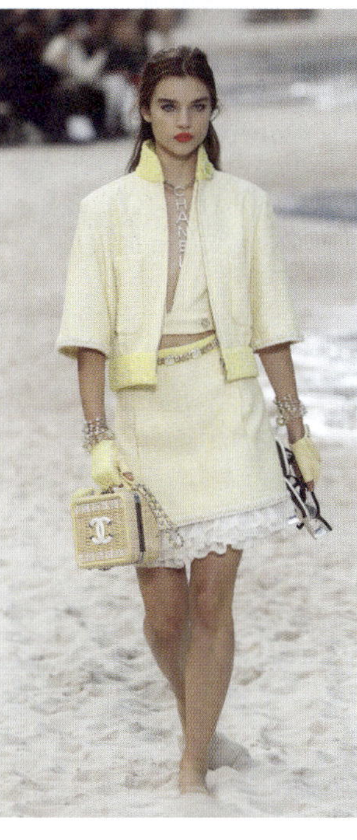

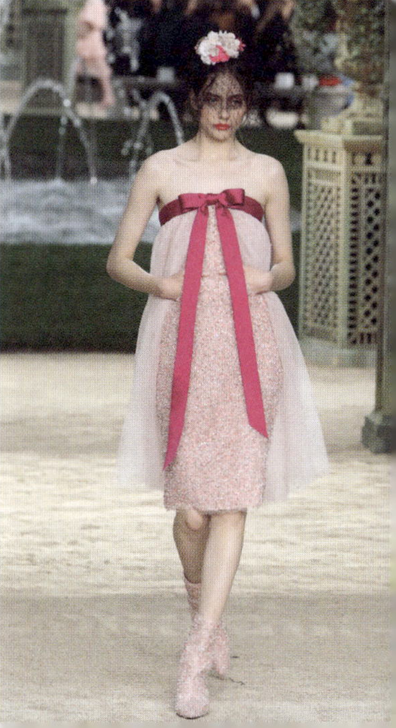

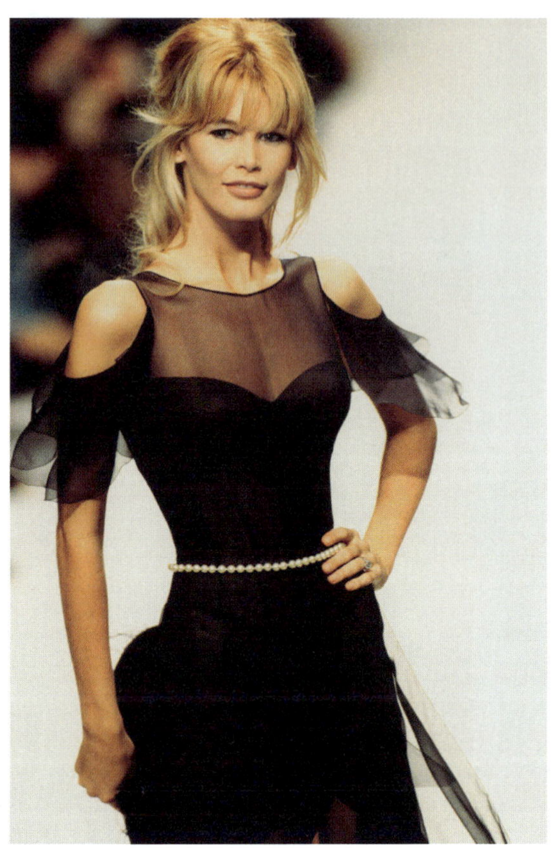

SPRING/SUMMER *1994*

Miniskirts, crop tops, and tailored jackets were all geared toward the younger generation just getting into Chanel. Another memorable show by Karl, this collection had some fun hip-hop influences, like bucket hats and gold chain belts. The skirts, as part of the traditional tweed suit, were much shorter, almost micro-minis. Top supermodels, such as Claudia Schiffer and Cindy Crawford, looked awesome in each of the styles, which were modern and whimsical with cool patterns and gold detailing. The bikinis featured in the collection even had jewel details and the double-C logo across the front.

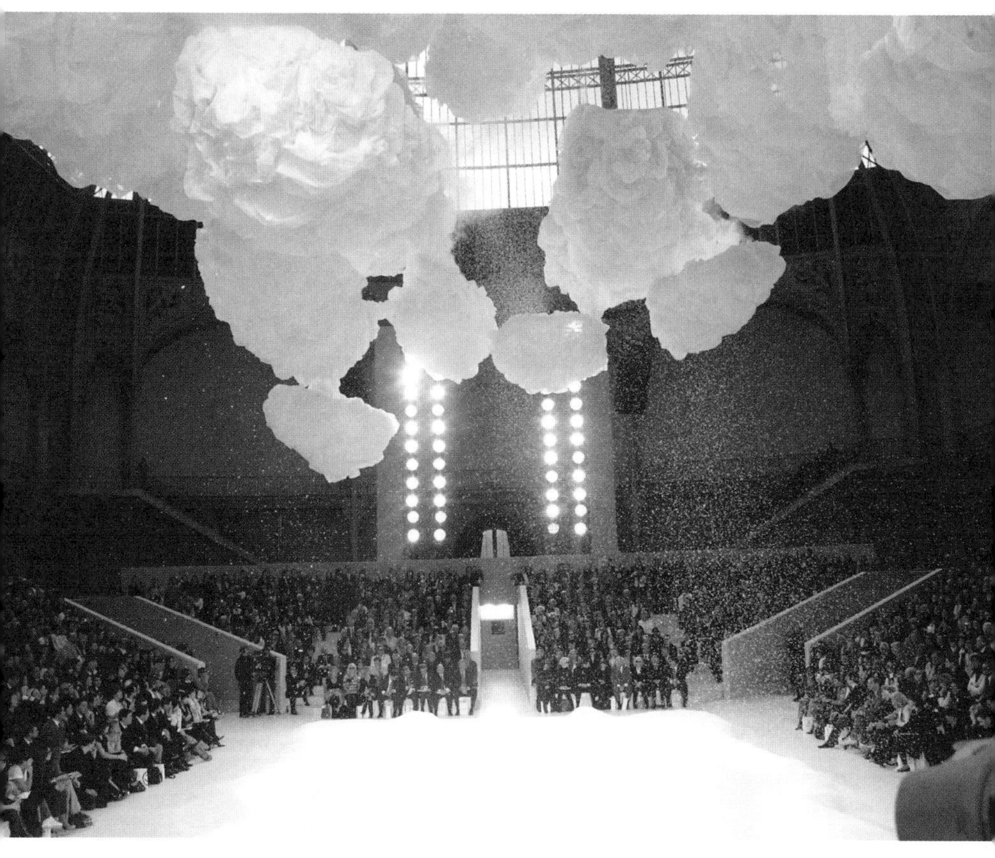

FALL/WINTER *2008*

Held at the Grand Palais in Paris, France, the runway show for this ready-to-wear collection was a smashing success. Karl debuted looks that had high-necked blouses, delicate knits, peplum jackets, and longer skirts. While it wasn't necessarily breaking any barriers, it was on trend for the time and was simply a beautiful, easy-to-wear collection. One of the most interesting updates he did was on the tweed suit. In his "poverty de luxe" style, each of the tweed suits had threadbare elbows and artfully placed patches. Considering this show took place during the recession in the United States, it was a spot-on, intelligent commentary on the state of the country.

CRUISE
2015

This was a collection that Karl presented in Dubai. Elle described the entire event as "magical." The show took place in a huge tent with an artificial desert and a giant Chanel logo at the entrance. The clothes that went down the runway featured harem pants, bold prints, and navy blue dresses lit up with actual lights. It was incredibly cool and an interesting take on classic Chanel fashions.

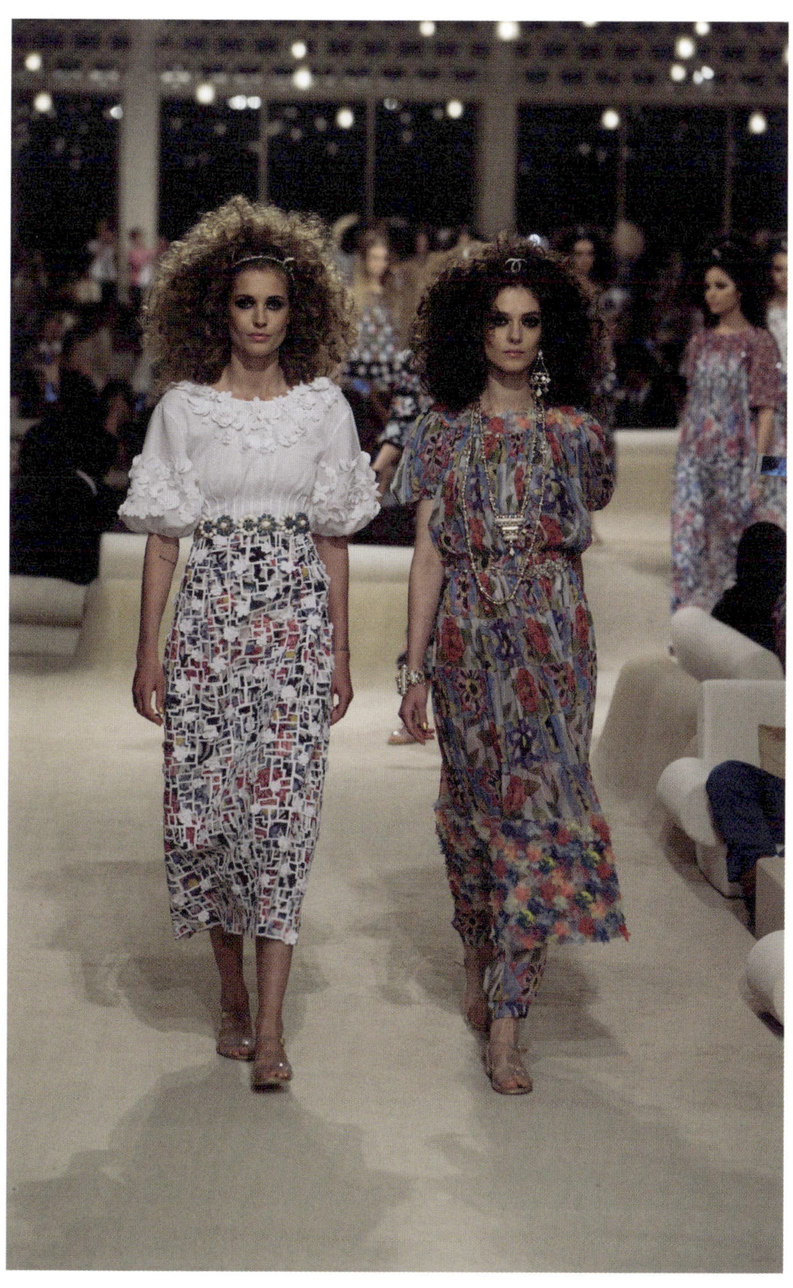

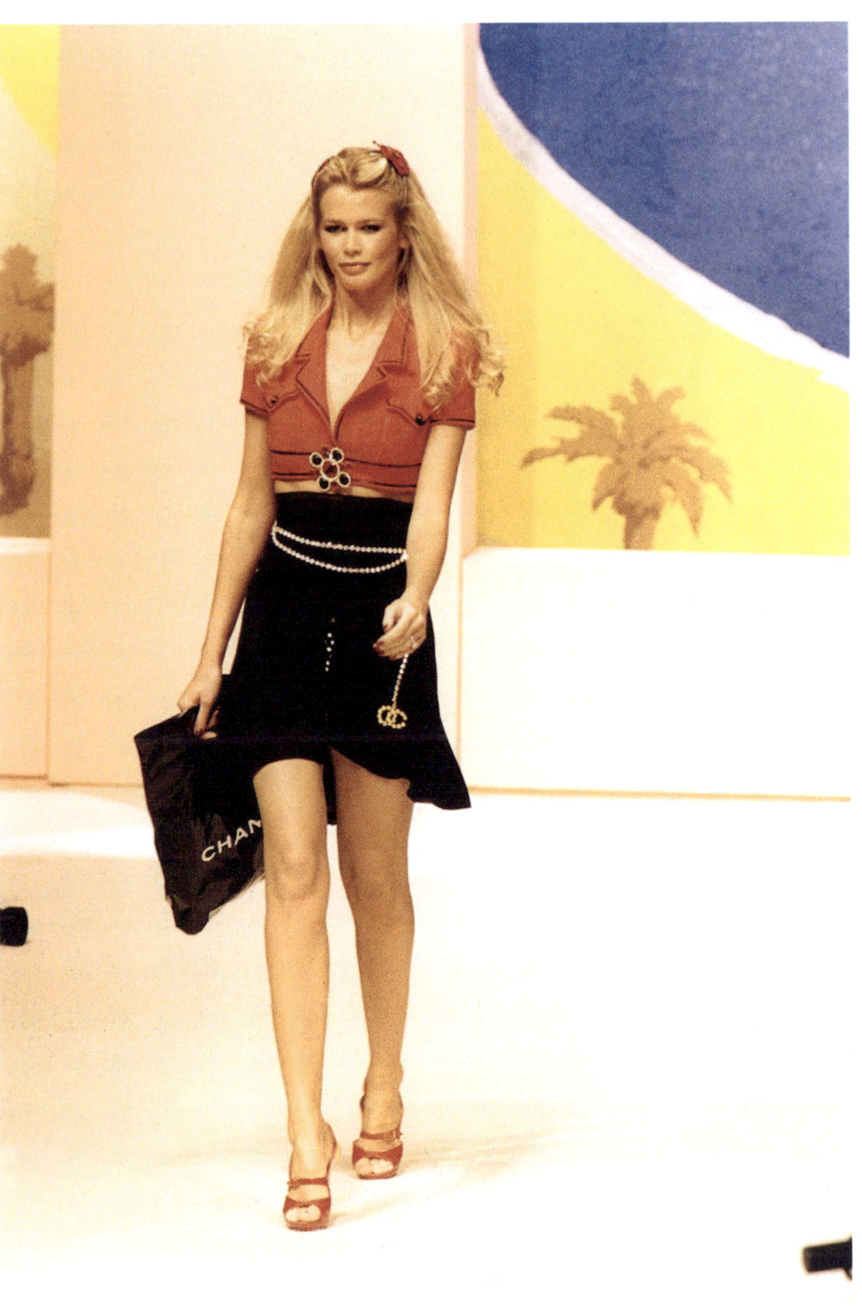
CHAN

“*CHANEL IS A TIMELESS BRAND THAT EPITOMIZES ELEGANCE AND SOPHISTICATION.* WORKING WITH CHANEL WAS ALWAYS A DREAM COME TRUE *FOR ME AS A MODEL.*”

Claudia Schiffer

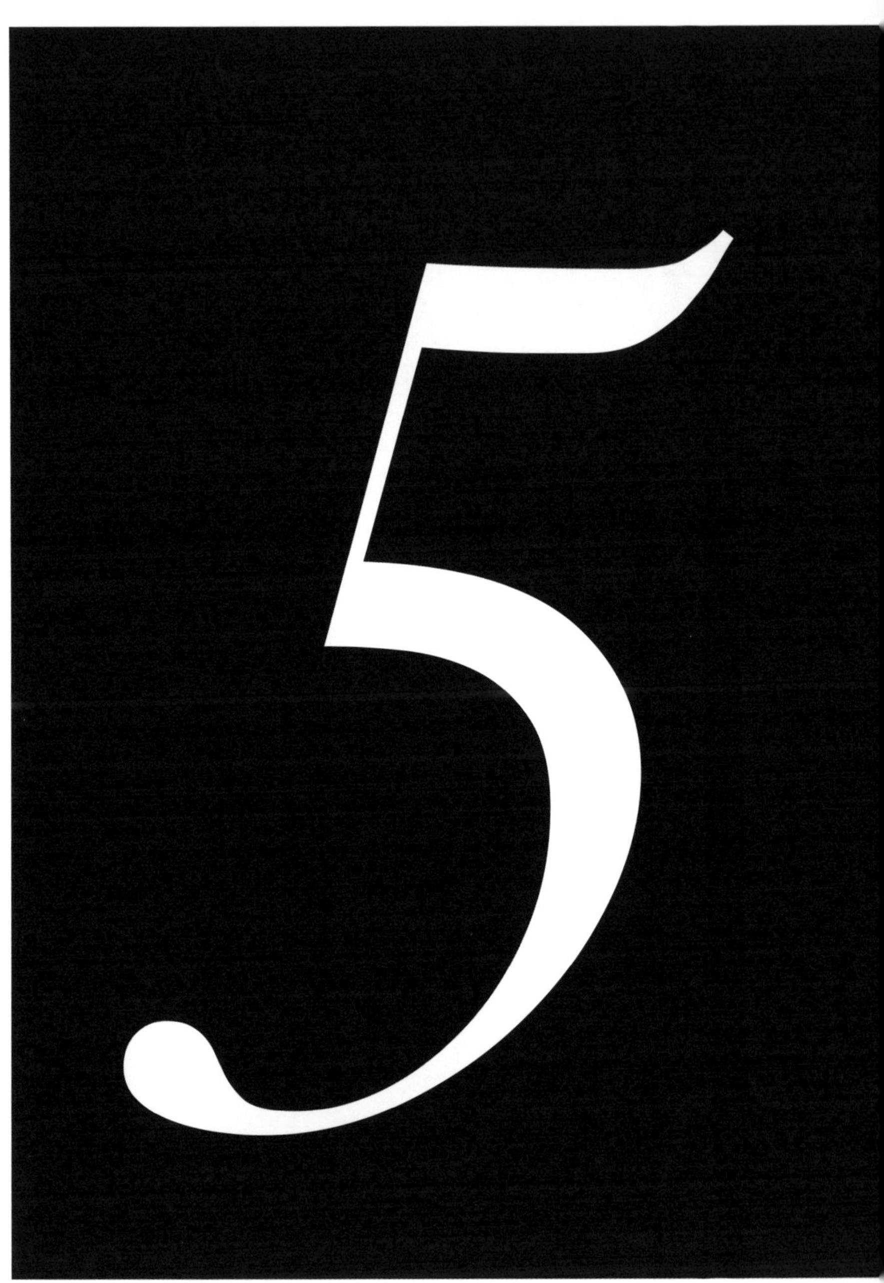

CHANEL N°5 *Is a* FRAGRANCE GAME CHANGER

Fragrance

CHANEL N°5 IS A FRAGRANCE THAT CHANGED THE WORLD. The mystique of this scent is legendary. Created by Coco Chanel in 1921, it was meant to be given to her best clients as a gift. Eventually, the popularity of the fragrance led her to sell it in her boutiques with much success. If you have ever smelled Chanel N°5, you know how memorable the scent can be. It's a classic, has massive staying power, and celebrates the female spirit. So, what are the notes in Chanel N°5? As a classic floral fragrance, some of the top notes are ylang-ylang and neroli, with jasmine and lily of the valley in the middle and sandalwood as the base. It's a truly elegant fragrance and is considered a masterpiece.

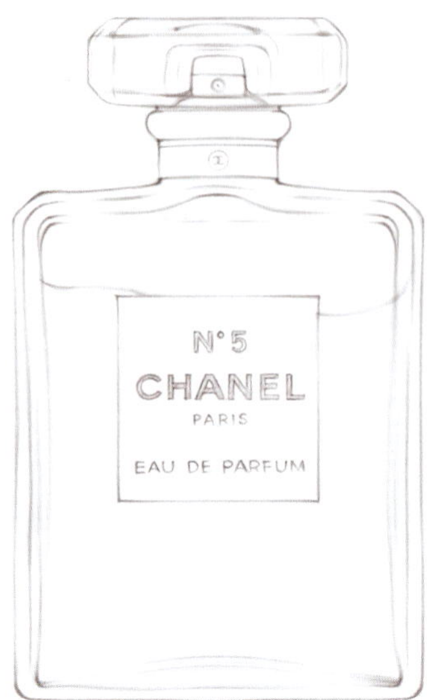

Coco felt that the number five was lucky. She not only received Chanel N°5 as the fifth fragrance sample from the perfumer but usually presented her collections in the fifth month of the year, May. Therefore, Chanel N°5 became the simple yet unforgettable name.

The bottle's design is just as elegant as the fragrance. Coco didn't want it to be too flashy or over the top, like many of the perfume bottles back then. She wanted a clear bottle to showcase the fragrance's gold color. Some say that the bottle looks like a whiskey decanter, which might have been what inspired Coco. The bezel-cut stopper and rectangular shape of the bottle have changed slightly over the years, but the fragrance is still recognizable. Artist Andy Warhol even immortalized the bottle in his pop artwork Ads: Chanel, printed on silk screen.

In another famous moment, Marilyn Monroe once said in an interview, "What do I wear to bed? Well, Chanel N°5, of course." There is a well-known photograph of Marilyn at the Ambassador Hotel in New York City getting ready, dabbing a bit of the fragrance on her decolletage while wearing a sparkling gown. The photograph has been used many times in Chanel ads.

Millennials and Gen Z may associate Chanel N°5 with their grandmothers, but today, it's becoming cool to wear retro fragrances again. Here are some of the other best-selling Chanel fragrances from over the years that are still sold today.

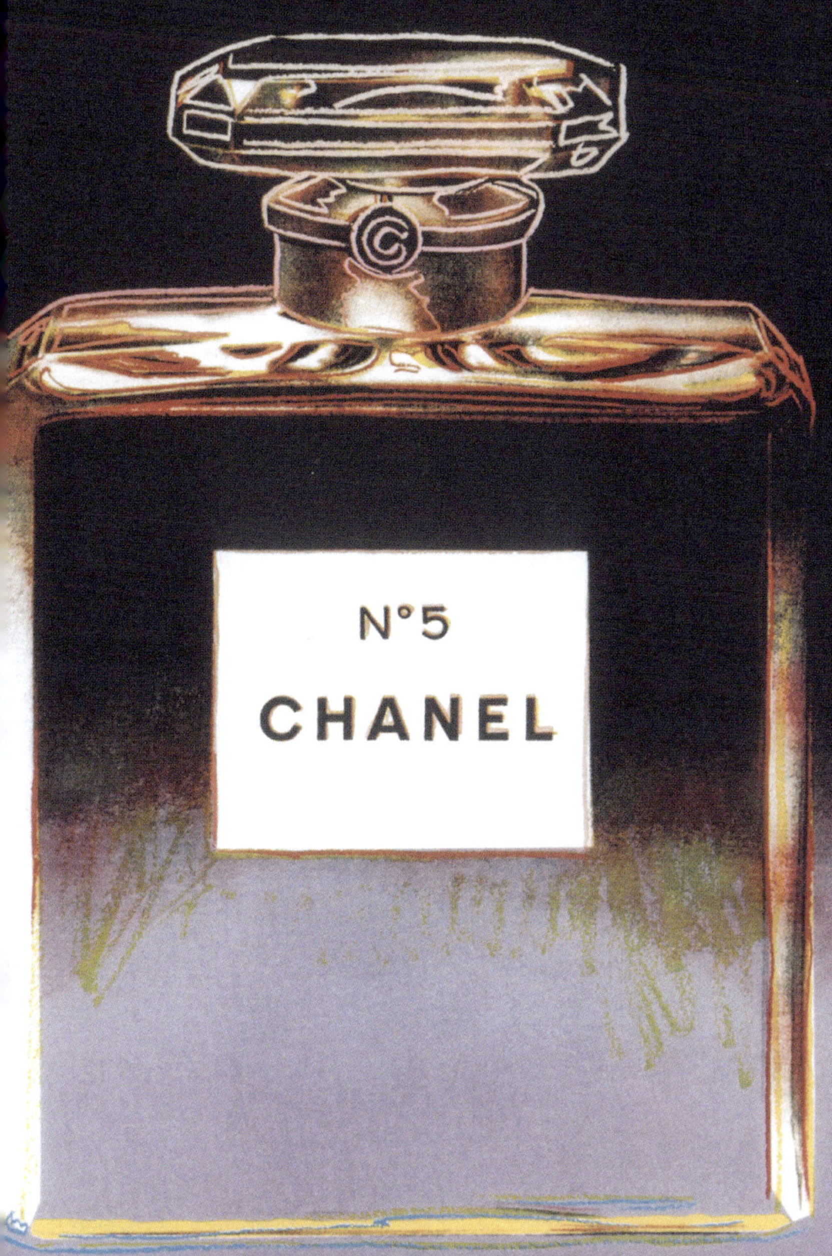
N°5
CHANEL
THE MOST TREASURED NAME IN PERFUME
HANEL

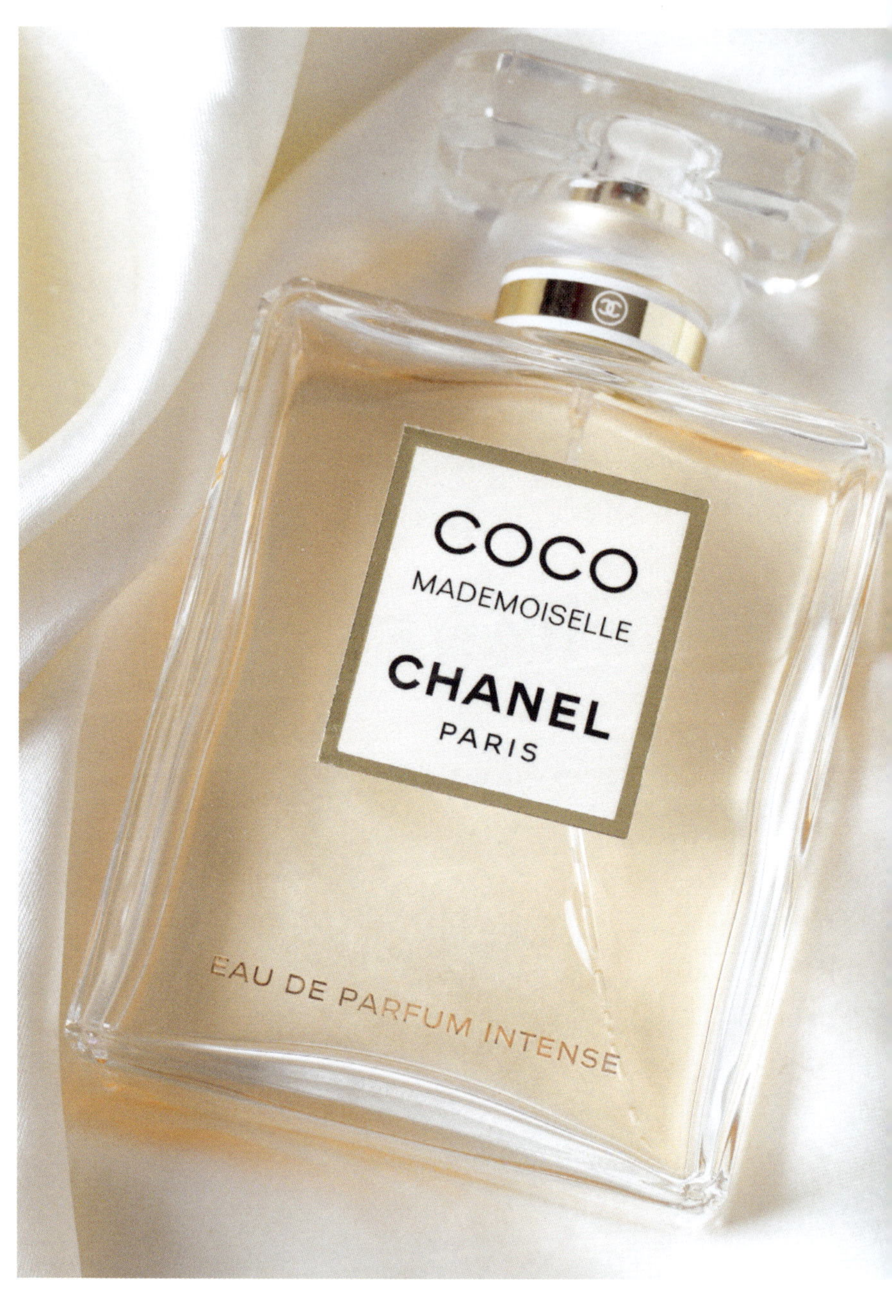
COCO
MADEMOISELLE
CHANEL
PARIS
EAU DE PARFUM INTENSE

Coco Mademoiselle

Coco Mademoiselle is a fresh, amber fragrance that is modern and youthful. It was created in 2001 for the younger Chanel clientele. The scent was created by Jacques Polge, head perfumer from 1978 to 2015 and considered "the nose" of Chanel. Sparkling and light, with a peach color and the same bottle shape as Chanel N°5, it's as though Coco Mademoiselle is the fun younger sister of the classic Chanel N°5. Orange, rose, patchouli, white musk, and vetiver are some of the notes in this woody floral fragrance.

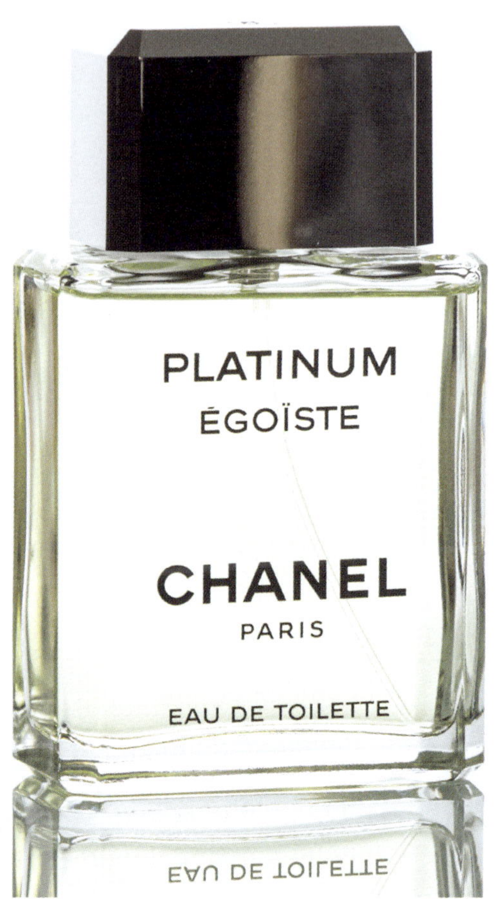

Égoïste

A bold and rich fragrance, Égoïste lives up to its name. In English, the word means "egoist," which is another term for a self-centered person. Sandalwood and ambrette seed are two of the main notes that give this men's fragrance an unmistakable masculinity. Warm, woody, and spicy, it's a traditional fragrance that demands to be worn by a strong man. This powerhouse was released in 1990.

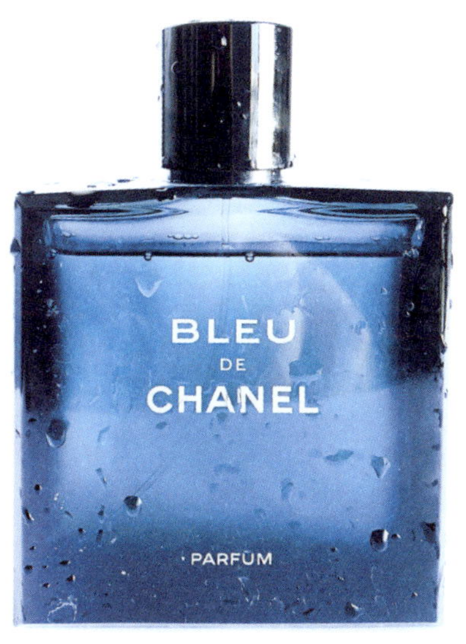

Bleu de Chanel

Bleu de Chanel is a clean, woody fragrance for men that came out in 2010. Chanel describes it as being "the spirit of a man who chooses his own destiny with independence and determination—a man who defies convention." So, in essence, Bleu de Chanel should be worn by a confident gentleman who appreciates notes of lemon, pepper, ginger, vanilla, and cedar.

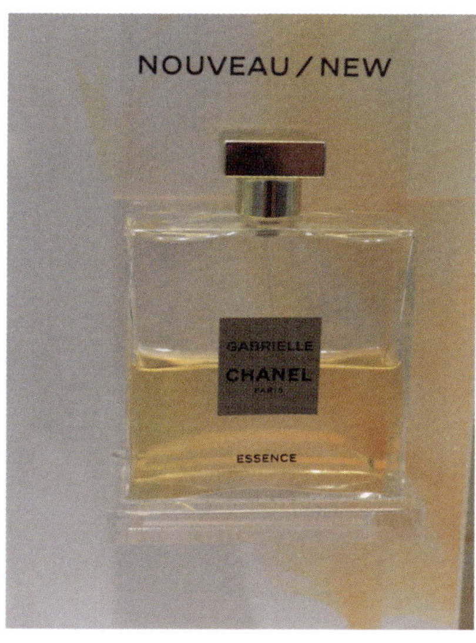

Gabrielle Chanel Essence

A crisp white floral scent forms the foundation of Gabrielle Chanel Essence. Honoring the birth name of the Chanel's founder, this fragrance came out in 2017 and features radiant floral notes of orange blossom, tuberose, and jasmine. It was created by Olivier Polge, current head of fragrance for Chanel and the son of the former head, Jacques. Clearly, superior noses run in the family.

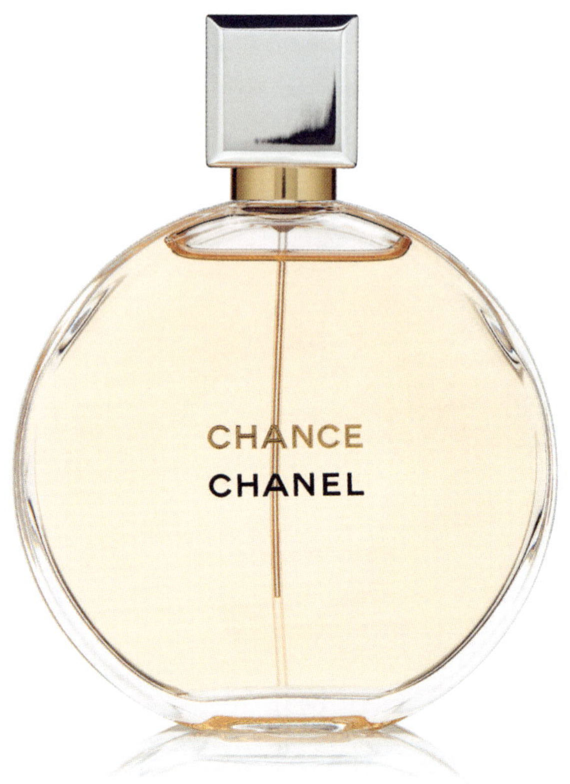

Chance

Chanel Chance came out in 2002 and was a surprising departure from the traditional Chanel fragrance. The bottle was round, while all other Chanel perfumes were square or rectangular. The House of Chanel has done quite a few different versions of Chance, like Chance Eau Tendre, Chance Eau Vive, and Chance Eau Fraîche, but the original is a floral scent featuring notes of iris, pink pepper, hyacinth, white musk, and jasmine.

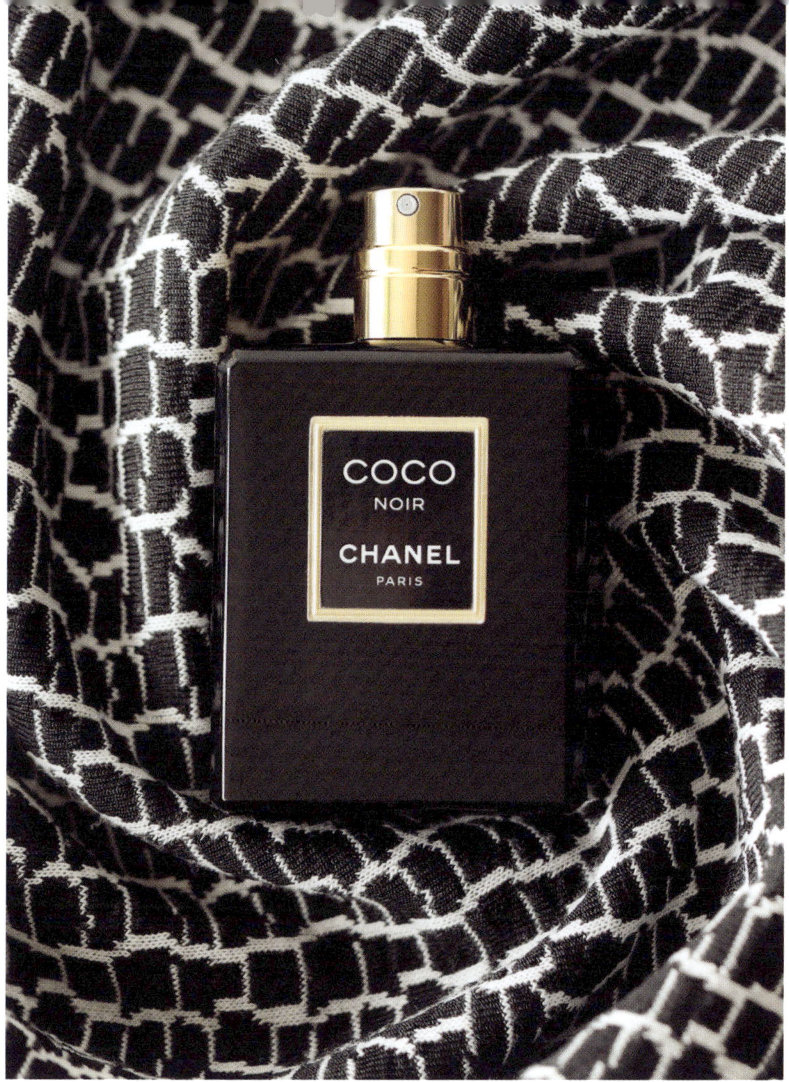

Coco Noir

Coco Noir is a woody, amber fragrance that comes off as quite spicy. It was launched in 2012 with notes of Calabrian bergamot, narcissus, tonka bean, and white musk frankincense. When Jacques created it, he wanted it to be worn at night by adventurous women who liked to look up at the stars. Warm and sexy, some fragrance connoisseurs compare it to Magie Noire, one of Lancôme's most famous scents. The bottle is a dramatic, opaque black with the same shape and dropper as Chanel N°5.

Allure

Rose, vanilla, and mandarin come together in a symphony of elegance for this women's fragrance, which came out in 1996. Two years later, Chanel released an Allure Homme for men. The women's version instantly became a bestseller in the late 1990s. People loved how unique, bright, and modern the Allure fragrance was in comparison to heavier Chanel scents, such as N°5.

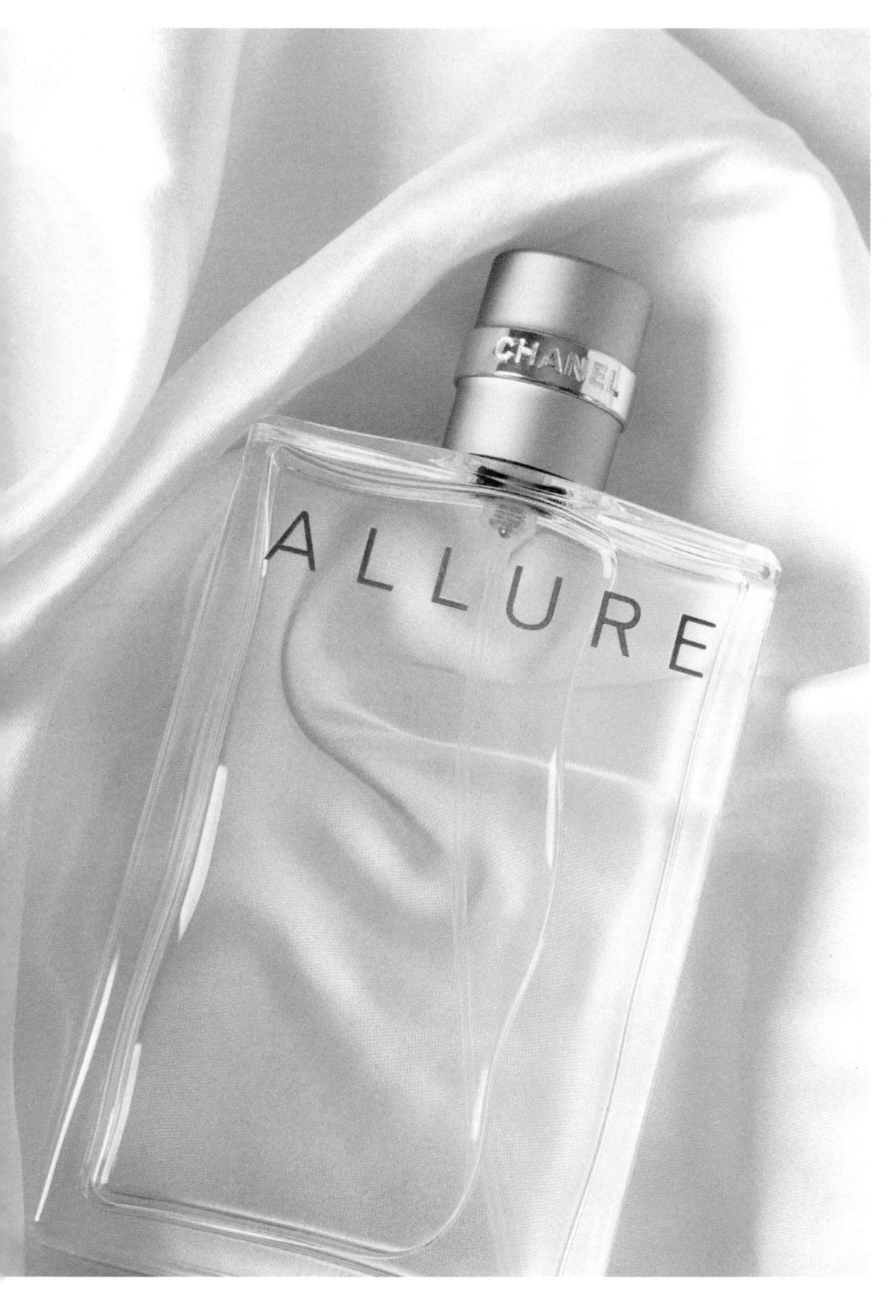
CHANEL
ALLURE

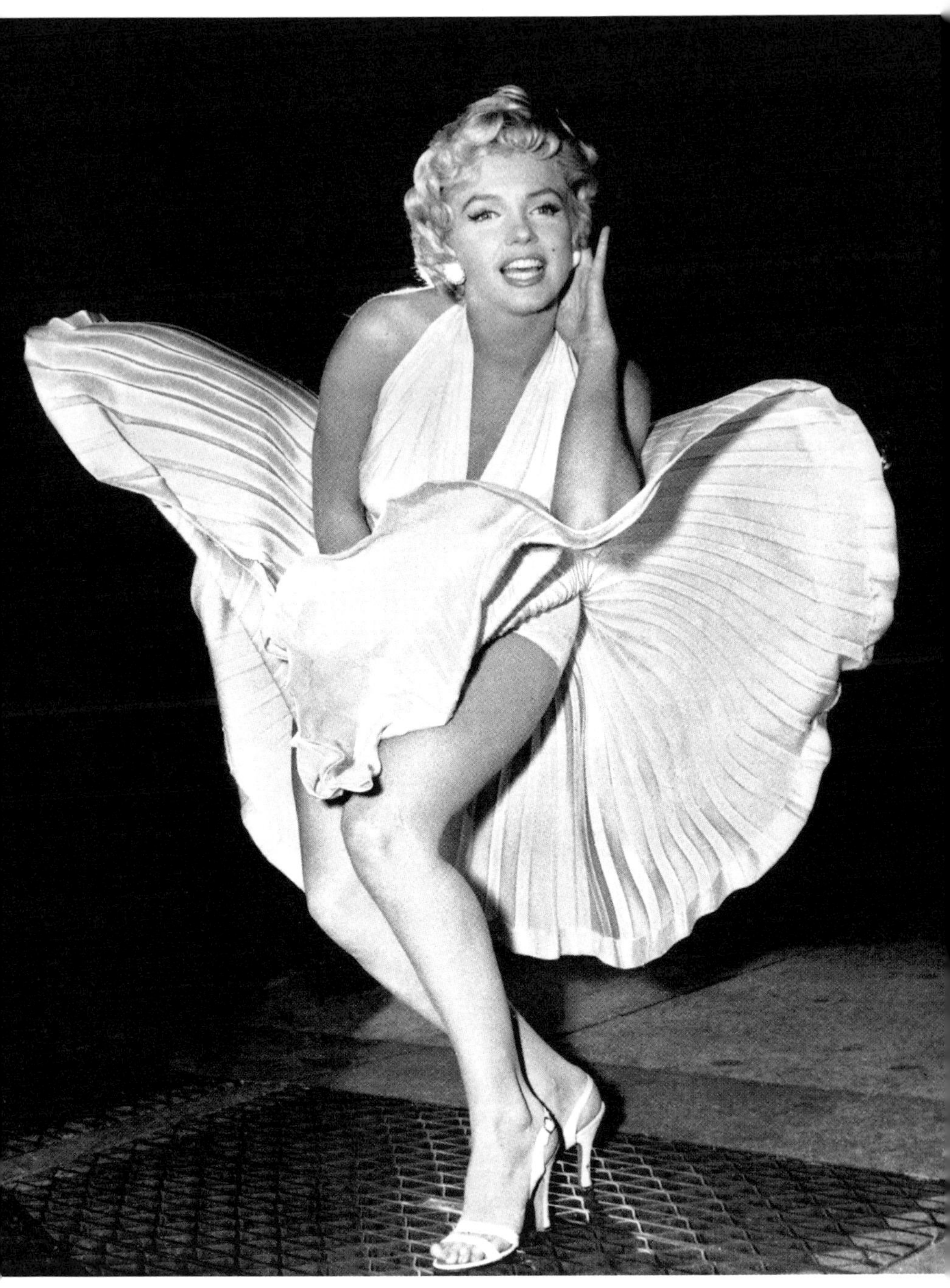

“WHAT DO I WEAR IN BED? WHY, CHANEL NO. 5, OF COURSE.”

Marilyn Monroe

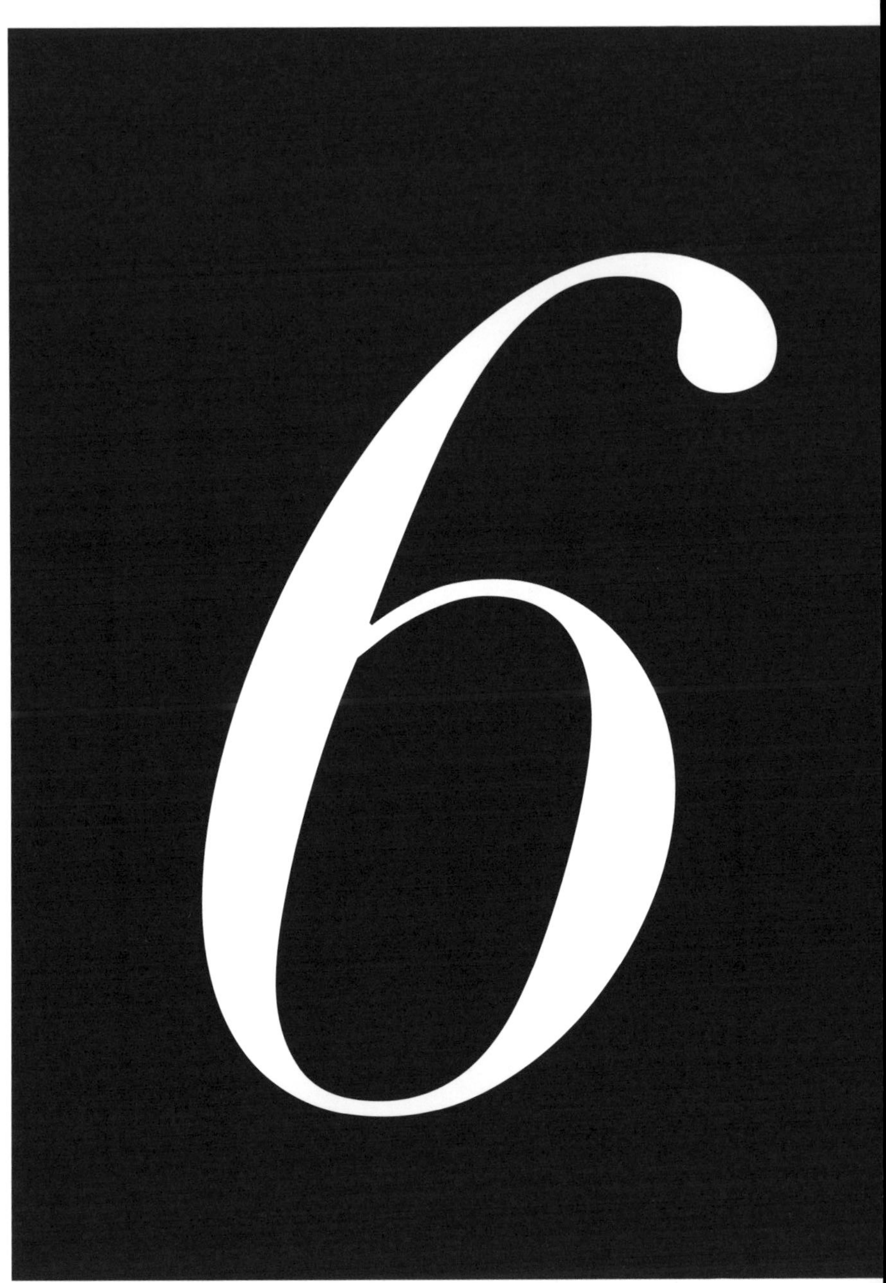

IT ALL BEGAN WITH THE *CHANEL 2.55*

Handbags

THE LOOK OF A QUILTED CHANEL HANDBAG is unmistakable. When you carry one, you are holding a piece of fashion history. Coco Chanel herself developed the first Chanel handbag in 1929. Most of the handbags that women carried at the time were clutches that didn't have straps. Inspired by the handles on a soldier's bag, she decided to put thin straps on a small rectangular bag and began to sell it in her boutique. It was a huge success.

T

he handbag got an update in 1955, specifically in February, and the new version was called Chanel 2.55 for the year and the month in which it was created. Over the years there have been many incarnations of the handbag, including different fabrics, styles, colors, and detailing.

The Chanel 2.55 has some standard features. For example, the lining on the inside of the handbag is usually burgundy. Coco did this to honor the nuns who wore uniforms of that color in the convent where she was raised after her parents passed away.

On the inside flap of the bag, there is a zippered pouch. The history goes that this pouch is where Coco would store her love letters from her various romantic partners. And the most famous part of the bag is the quilted diamond-pattern material. There isn't a definitive answer on what inspired Coco to use this type of fabric, but some say she liked the details on the couch pillows in her Paris apartment, while others claim that she liked the quilting because it reminded her of the stained glass in churches.

The original version of the Chanel 2.55 had a lock on the front that Coco called the "mademoiselle lock." This was a clever reference to the fact that Coco never became anyone's wife. Today, the bag has a modern flap lock that fastens on its own when the bag is shut, with the double-C logo on the closure instead of a lock.

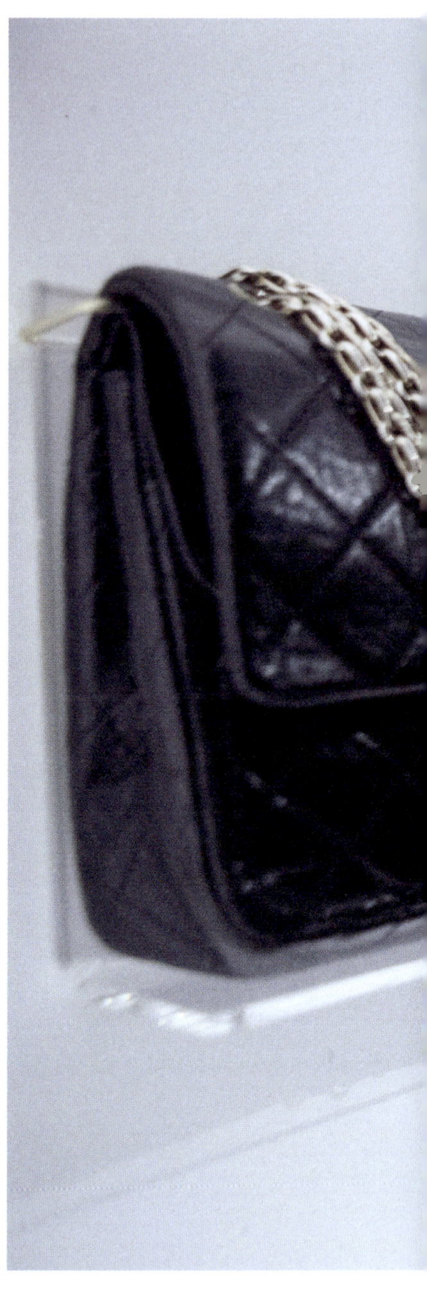

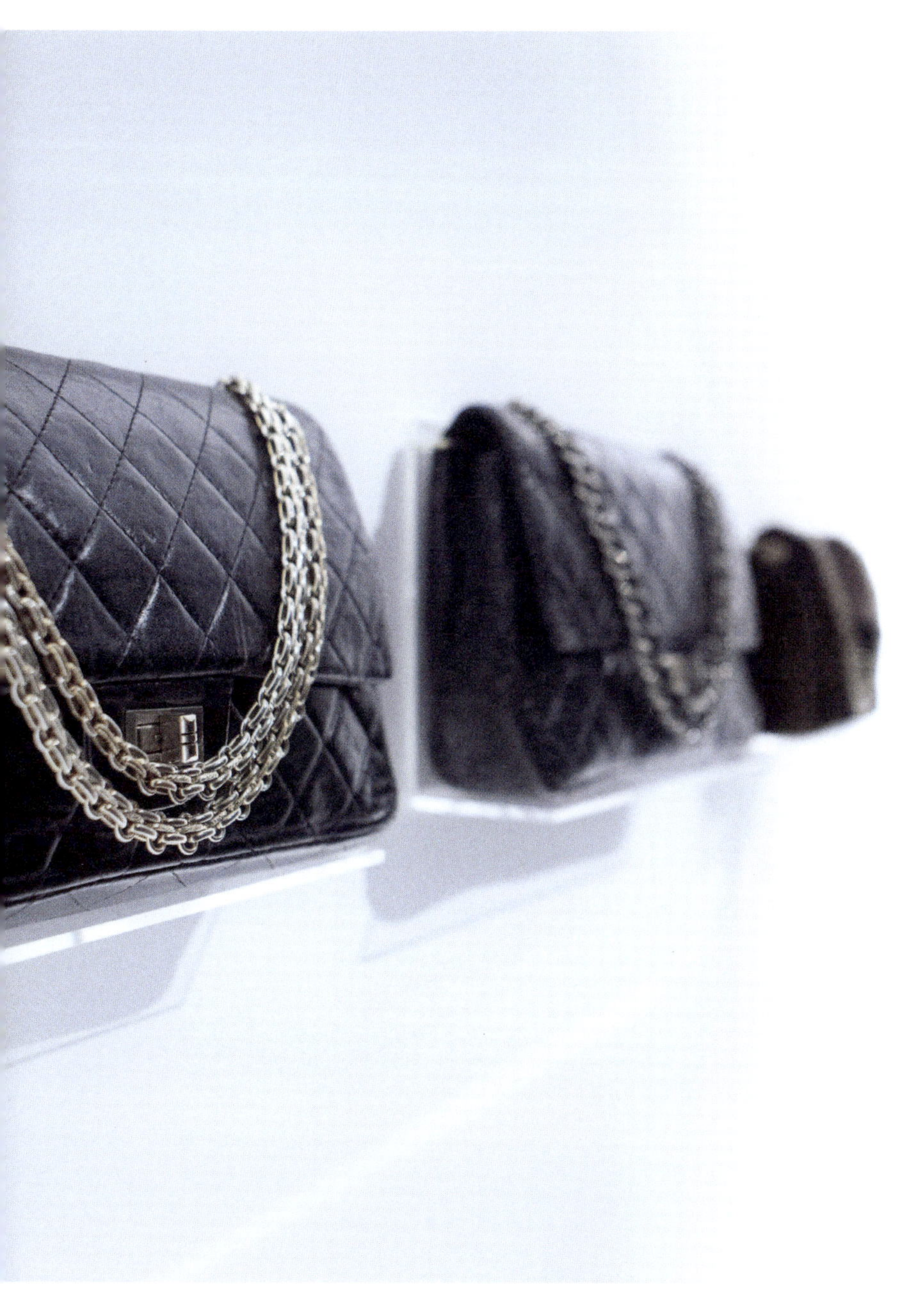

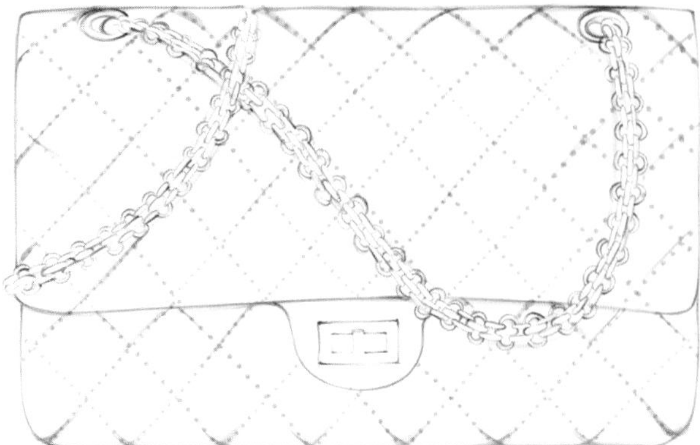

1955
The Chanel 2.55 bag was first introduced by Coco Chanel in February 1955, hence the name "2.55." It was designed to be both elegant and practical, revolutionizing women's handbag. design.

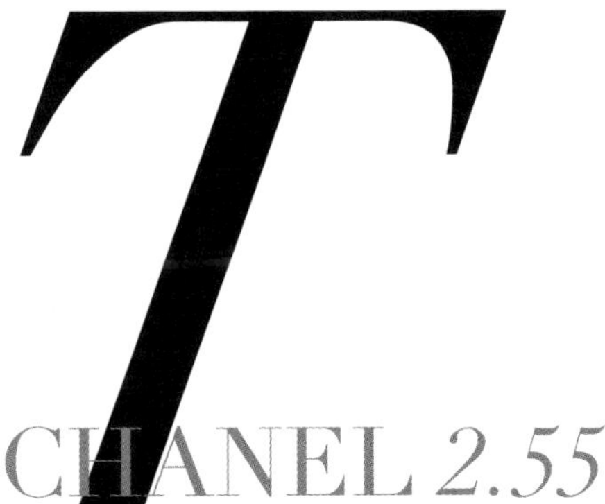

CHANEL *2.55*

This unique bag, which is still made today, is significant to the House of Chanel. Currently on the website, there is an ad about the bag featuring Penelope Cruz and Brad Pitt. Shot in various locations in Deauville, France, the bag is prominently featured. In the first scene, a black Chanel 2.55 is sitting on a table outside a café where the two actors are seated. While only 57 seconds long, the mini-film is based on a French movie called A Man and a Woman. The handbag is on display throughout, even tossed casually on the dashboard of the car the actors are driving. It's a chic ad featuring two of the biggest stars in the world and one of the most famous handbags ever made.

Of course, the Chanel 2.55 isn't the only popular handbag the House of Chanel has released over the years. Here are some of the others that have become staples of the fashion set all over the world.

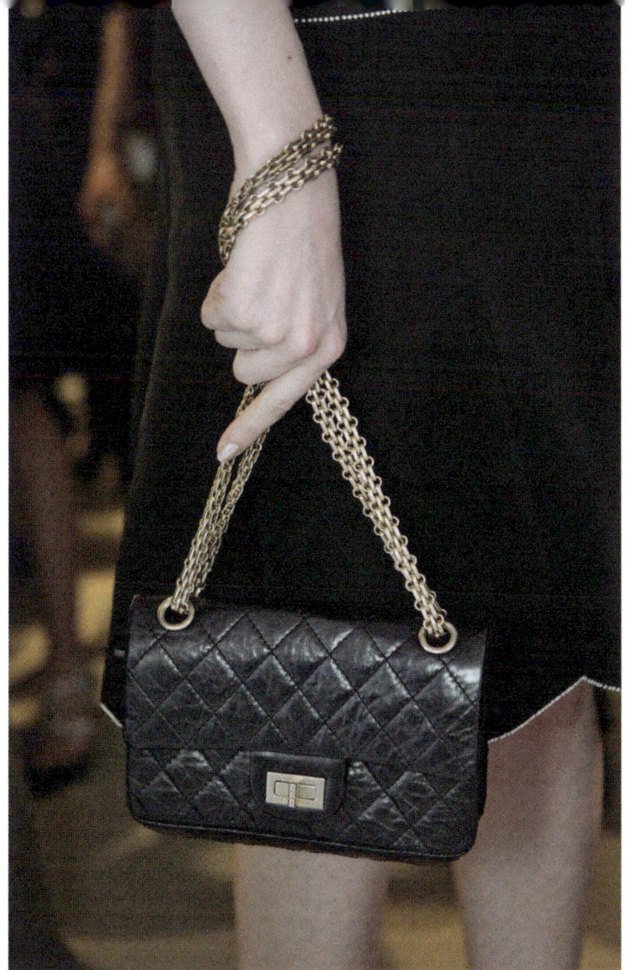

THE *2005* CHANEL *2.55*

This bag deserves special mention because it was released by Karl Lagerfeld in 2005 for the 50th anniversary of the Chanel 2.55 handbag. The fun detail they brought back for this version of the bag was the "mademoiselle lock." You can still buy this handbag with the turn lock today in a variety of sizes, from mini to large, and different fabrics, such as leather, tweed, or wool. There is a French message inside the bag that reads, "Cherie amie, la mode se démode, le style jamais – Gabrielle Chanel." It's a famous quote by Coco, saying that fashion goes out of date, but style never does.

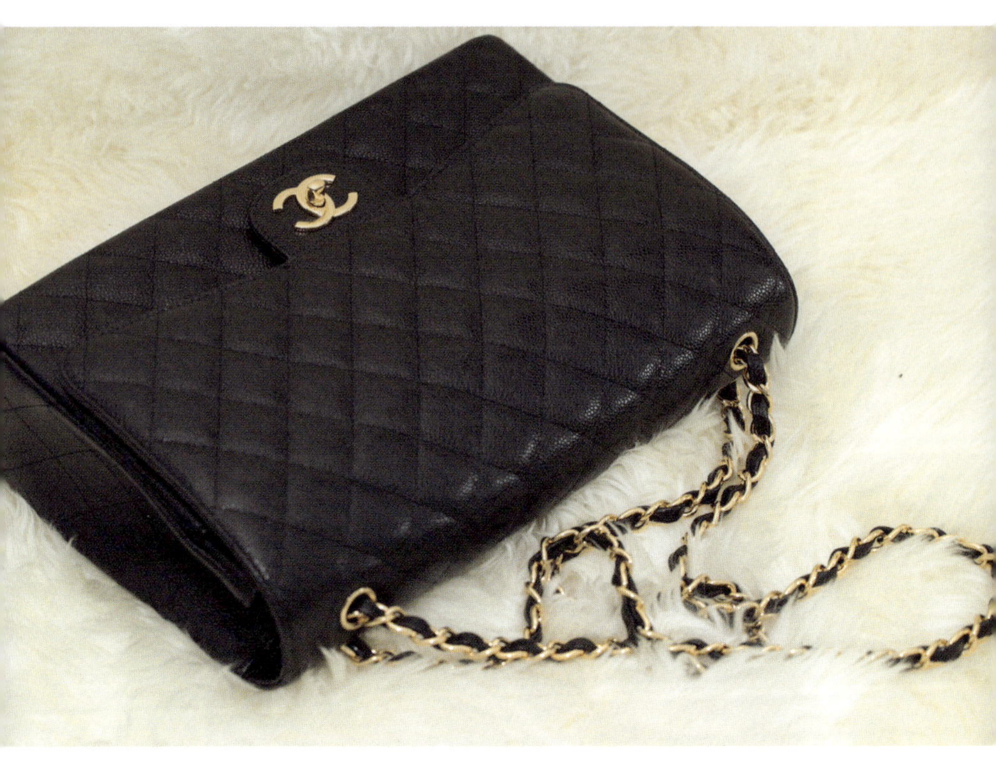

THE CLASSIC *11.12*

The Chanel Classic, or the 11.12 as it's called for the date it was created, is very similar to the Chanel 2.55. The design has single and double flap versions, comes in different sizes, and features classic and seasonal colors. The newest collection for Spring 2024 features the Classic 11.12 in lambskin with gold tone accents and a gorgeous pink and orange ombré color. The color is so beautiful that it's like watching the sun rise at the beach, perfect for spring.

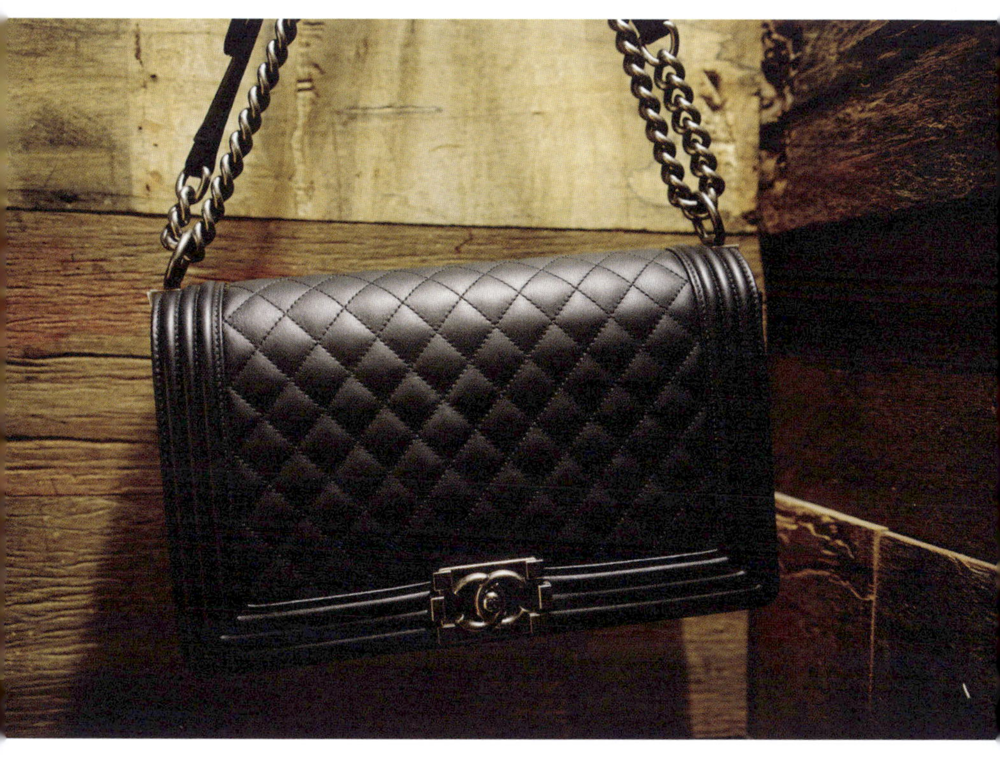

CHANEL BOY

The Chanel Boy bag first came out in 2011 when Karl was still creative director. It's a modern take on the Classic handbag with a large link chain and a boxier style. The look is meant to be unisex, and Karl named it for the first boy that Coco fell in love with, Captain Arthur Edward "Boy" Capel.

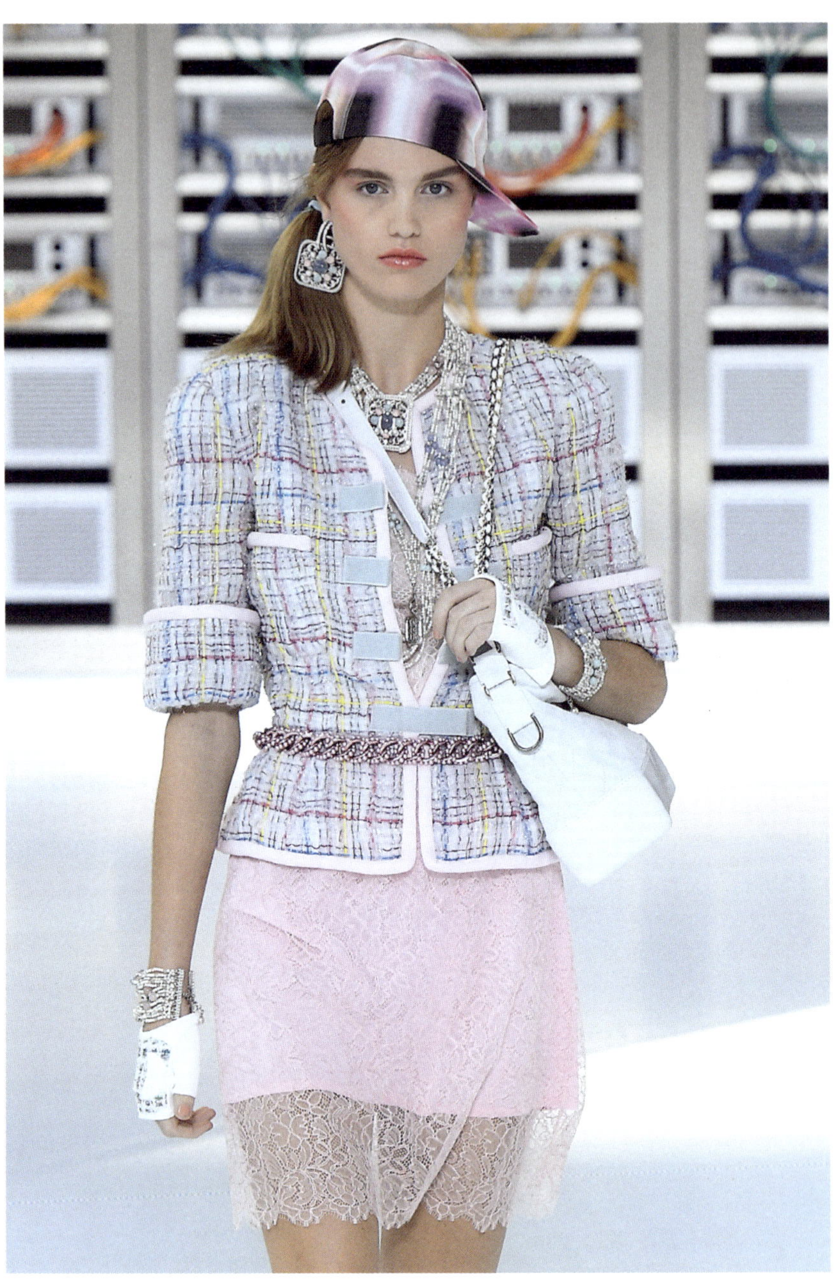

CHANEL GABRIELLE

This bag was named after the founder of Chanel. The bag is a more casual style than the structured Classic or 2.55 handbags. It comes in two styles, hobo or backpack, and was released in 2017, making it one of the newest styles available.

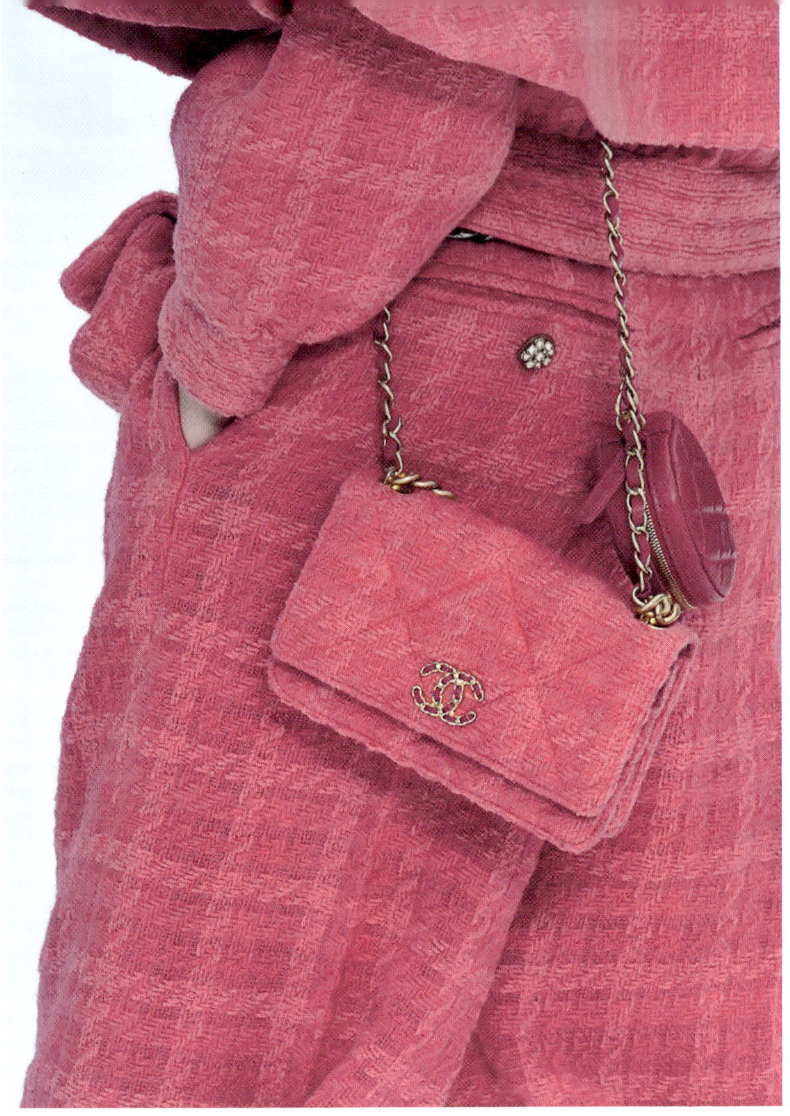

CHANEL *19*

The Chanel 19 is significant for being the last handbag that Karl designed before he passed away in 2019. The distinguishing features of this bag are its puffier look and the three strap chains. The overall design is still similar to the 2.55, but it has the iconic Chanel logo on the front.

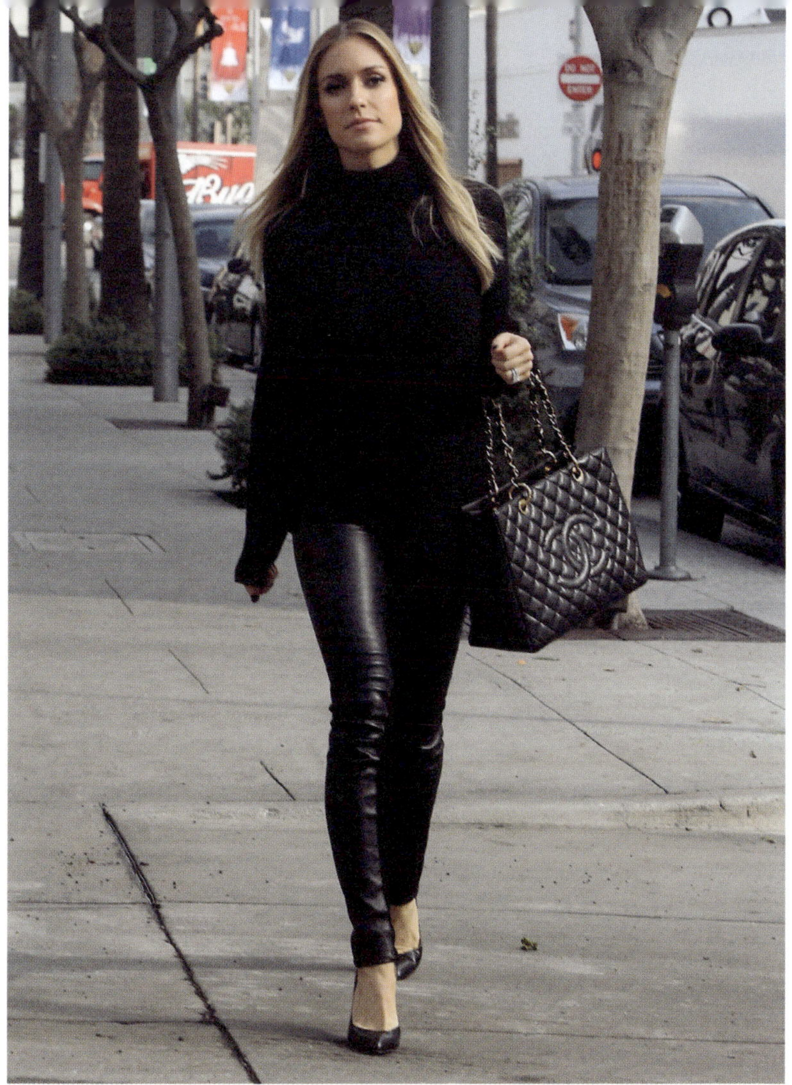

CHANEL GRAND SHOPPING TOTE

When you need to carry more than your Chanel 2.55 will hold, there is the famous Chanel Grand Shopping Tote, or GST. They discontinued the GST in 2015, even though it was very popular. You can search online vintage stores and, if you're lucky, find an original one. They come in beautiful styles, including a fun one with shaded calfskin and silver-toned metal in purple, blue, and dark blue.

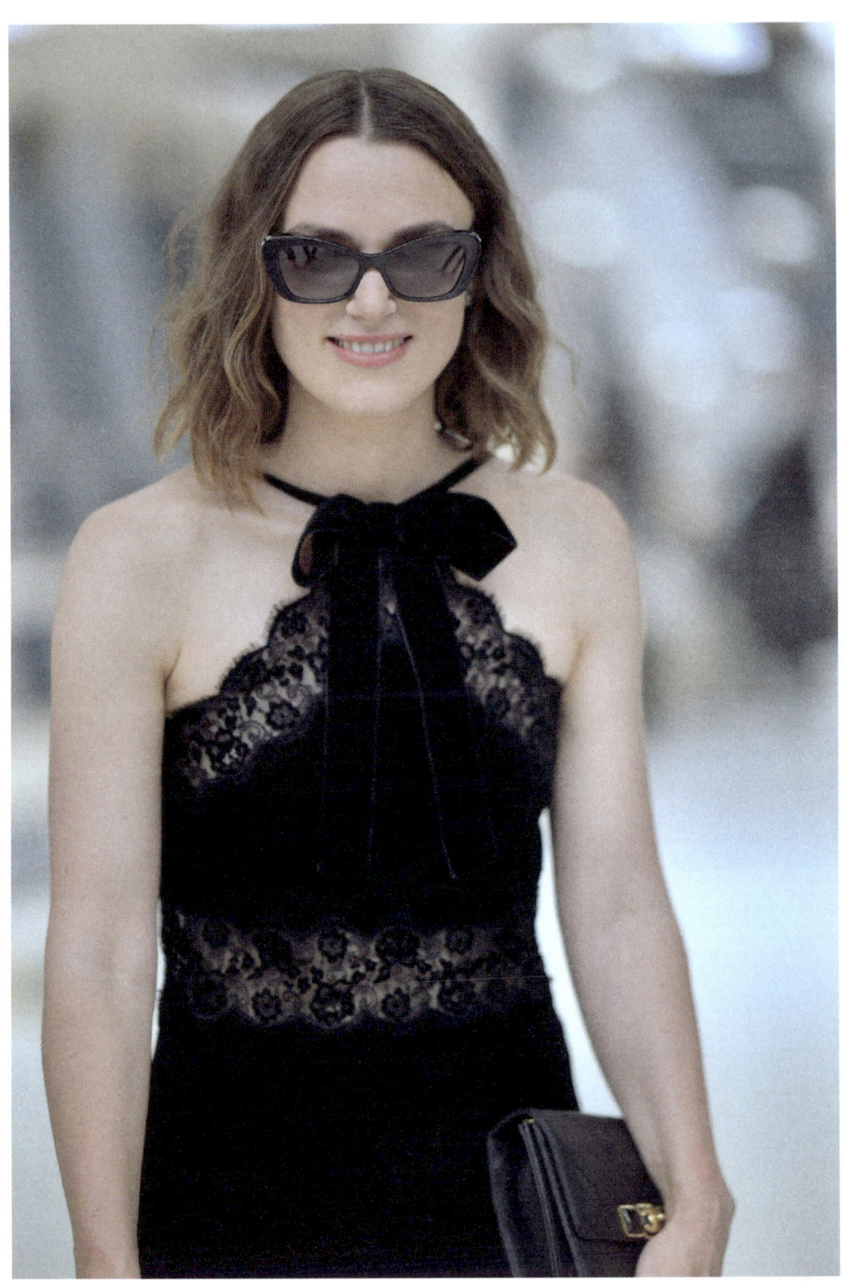

"I'VE ALWAYS LOVED CHANEL HANDBAGS. THEY'RE CLASSIC, TIMELESS, AND THEY GO WITH EVERYTHING."

Keira Knightley

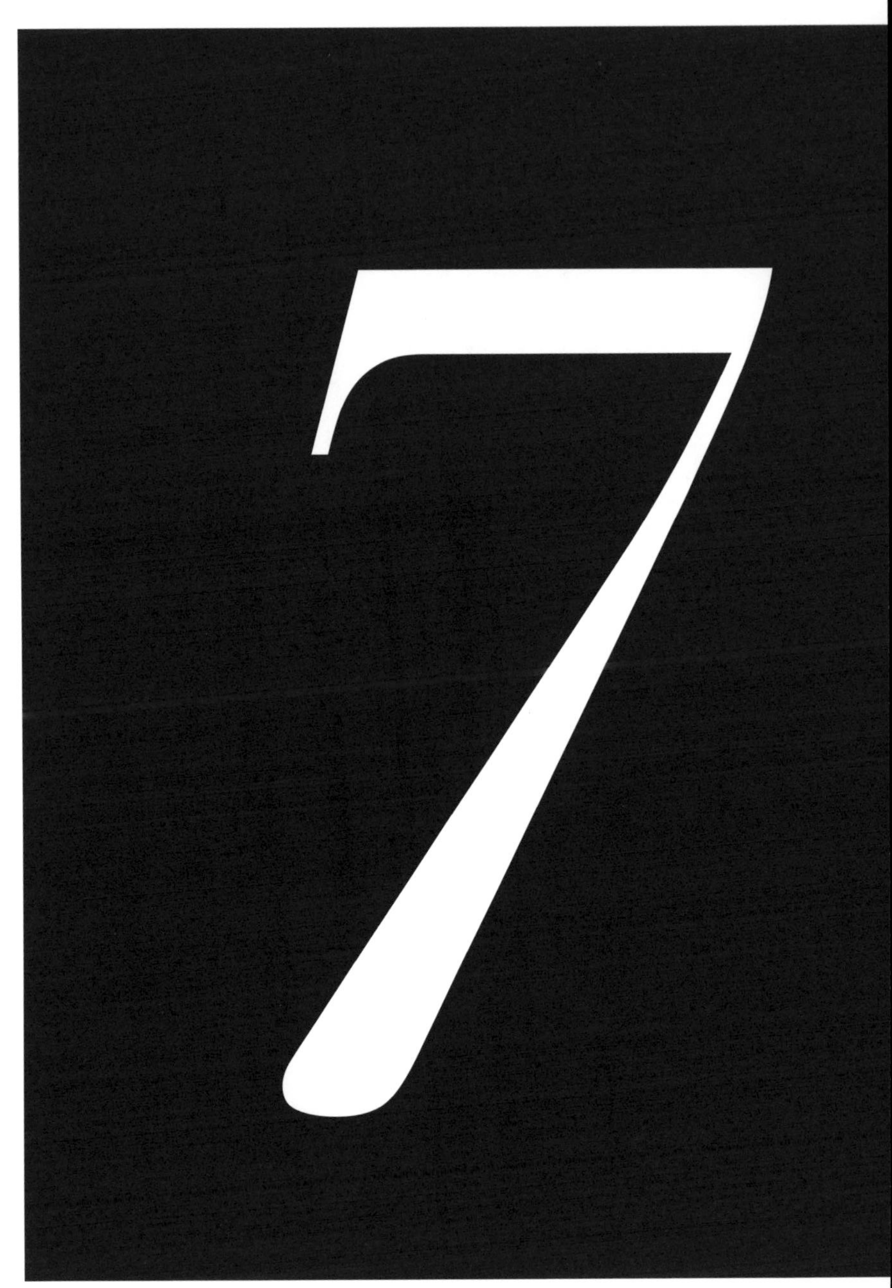

MAKING HEADLINES With *CHANEL*

In the news'

COCO CHANEL AND HER FASHION HOUSE weren't strangers to making headlines. When it comes to a world-renowned brand, being in the news is inevitable, whether it's for a good or a bad reason. There have been news stories over the years that have attracted attention and stirred up controversy, which hasn't always benefitted the brand. Let's explore some of the most interesting headlines involving Chanel throughout the decades.

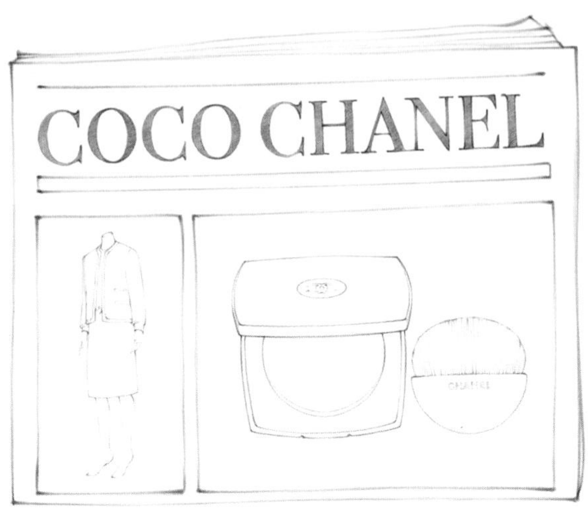

COCO *and* THE WAR

The first headline involves Coco herself. There is some evidence from declassified French documents suggesting that Coco was a spy for the Germans, which was shocking and a major scandal at the time. This happened in the 1940s, when the Nazis occupied Paris. Coco became close to a German military figure, Baron Hans Günther von Dincklage, and she moved into the Ritz Paris, which was where the German military officers were staying during the occupation.

The gossip was enough to make the news, but the real reason that Coco is thought to be a spy is because she was registered as "Agent F-7124." Though many believe that she was a "horizontal collaborator," Coco was never convicted of any crimes. During the war, she closed her stores but managed to relaunch the brand successfully in 1954. Coco continued to live at the Ritz Paris as a world-famous celebrity until she passed away in 1971.

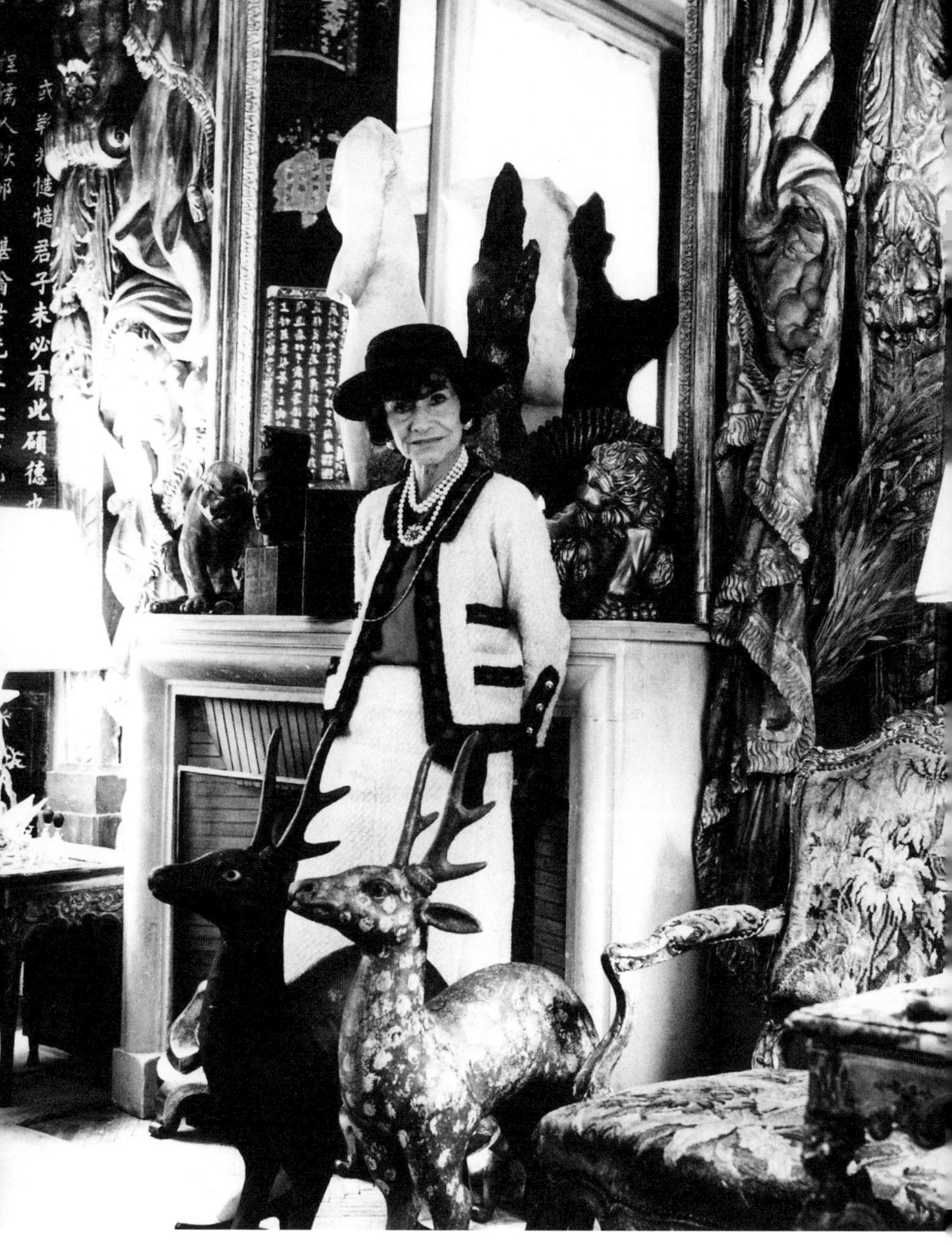

COCO AT RITZ

Coco Chanel lived in her grand suite at the Hotel Ritz in Paris for 30 years. The suite was filled with fashion, art, sculptures, and much more.

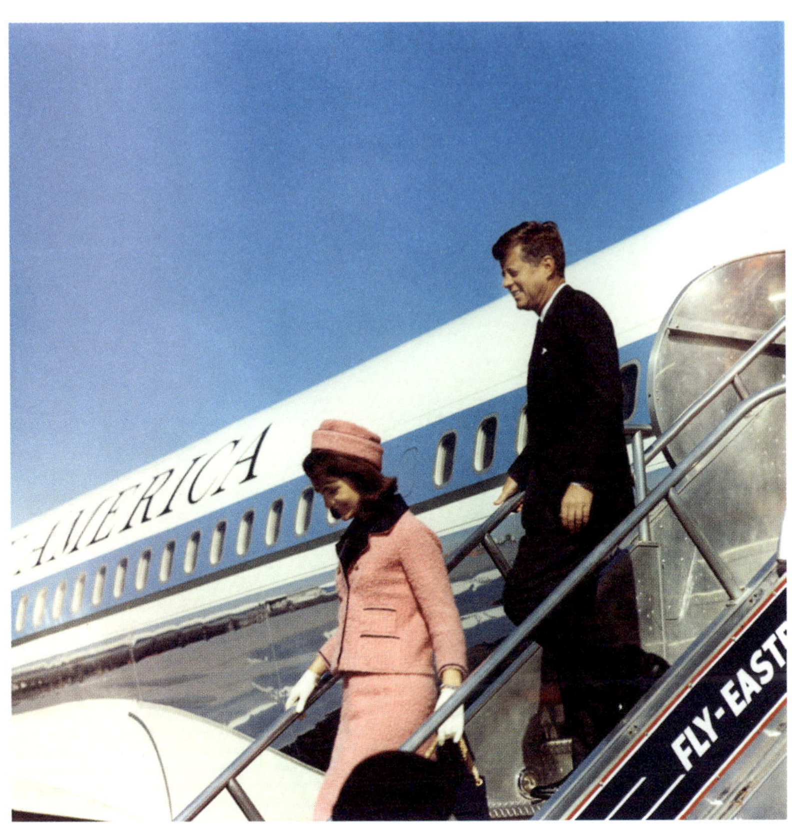

TRAGIC DAY

Jackie and John F. Kennedy arrive in Dallas, where the president is assassinated later that day.

JACKIE KENNEDY *and the* PINK CHANEL SUIT

It's one thing for a celebrity or politician to be photographed in Chanel, but it's a whole other thing for them to be photographed in that suit when the president of the United States is shot. On November 22, 1963, President John F. Kennedy was killed in Dallas, Texas, while riding in an open-air motorcade through the streets of the city. Jackie was seated next to her husband that tragic day, wearing a pink Chanel suit.

The suit was stained with blood, but Jackie insisted on not changing out of it before the swearing in of the next president of the United States, Lyndon B. Johnson. At the time, many of her staff tried to talk her into changing out of the suit, but Jackie replied, "Oh no, I want them to see what they have done to Jack." It's a morbid piece of history that Chanel became associated with. So, what happened to the suit?

After she took it off the next day, Jackie put it in a box with the date labeled on it. She sent it to her mother's house where it remained in the attic until it was given to the National Archives Building in College Park, Maryland. It was never cleaned or displayed and is kept in a preserved state in a secret location. Many films have depicted this tragic event, showing Jackie wearing the pink Chanel suit. Most recently, Natalie Portman played Jackie and wore an exact replica that the film's costume designer created. The buttons, gold chains, and Chanel logos were all provided to the costumer by the House of Chanel so that it would look authentic.

BANNING FUR *at* CHANEL

Chanel made headlines when it finally decided to ban fur in 2018. Many other fashion houses, such as Gucci, Versace, and Burberry, had already decided not to include fur in their lines anymore. Chanel banned not only fur but also exotic animal skins, including crocodile, lizard, snake, and stingray.

The nonprofit People for the Ethical Treatment of Animals, or PETA, supported this decision and had been responsible for much of the pressure put on Chanel to make this choice. The animal rights organization argued that there are many alternative materials, such as vegan leather and other faux fabrics, that work just as well as fur or exotic animal skins. Chanel agreed with them, and in fact had already begun using fake fur in some of their collections years earlier. In fact, the Fall/Winter 2010 show in Tokyo, Japan, showed off models in head-to-toe faux fur. Some of the faux fur was even woven into tweed, with vegan leather accents, to update the classic Chanel suit for the arctic style.

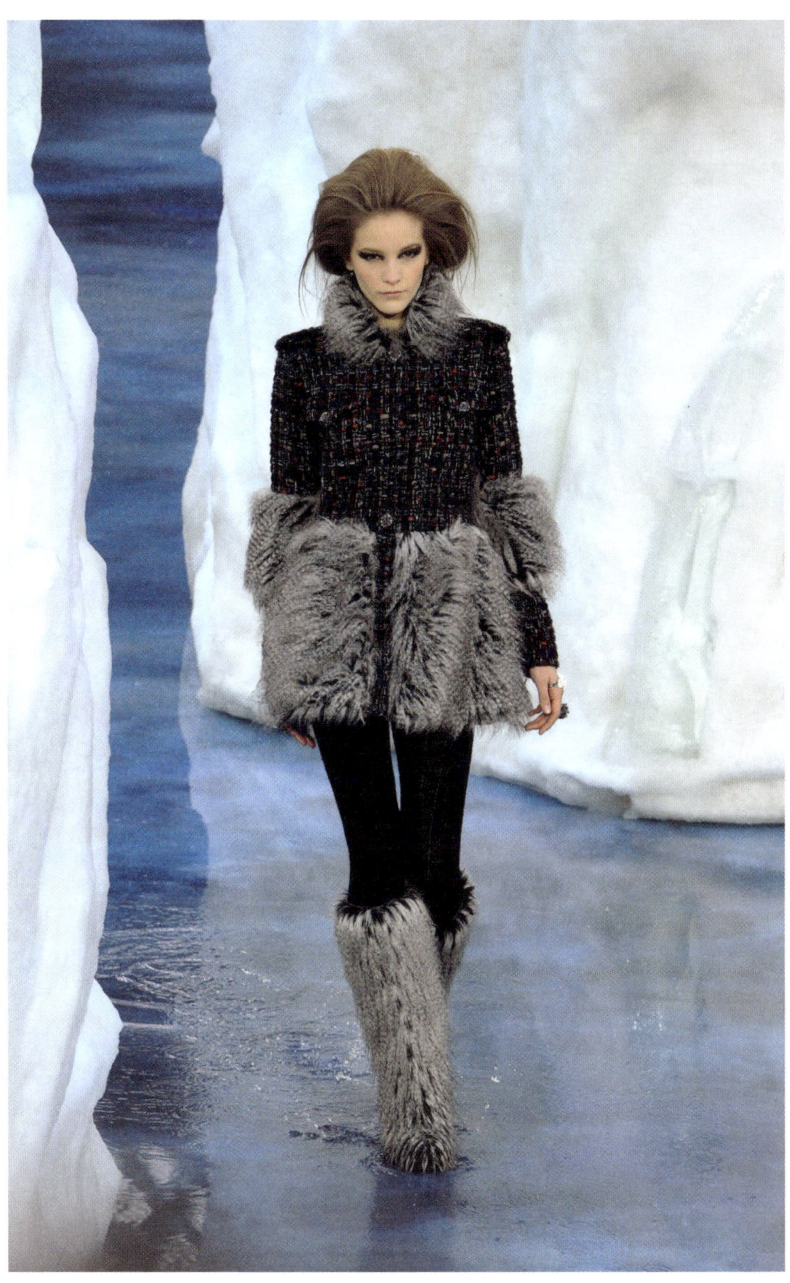

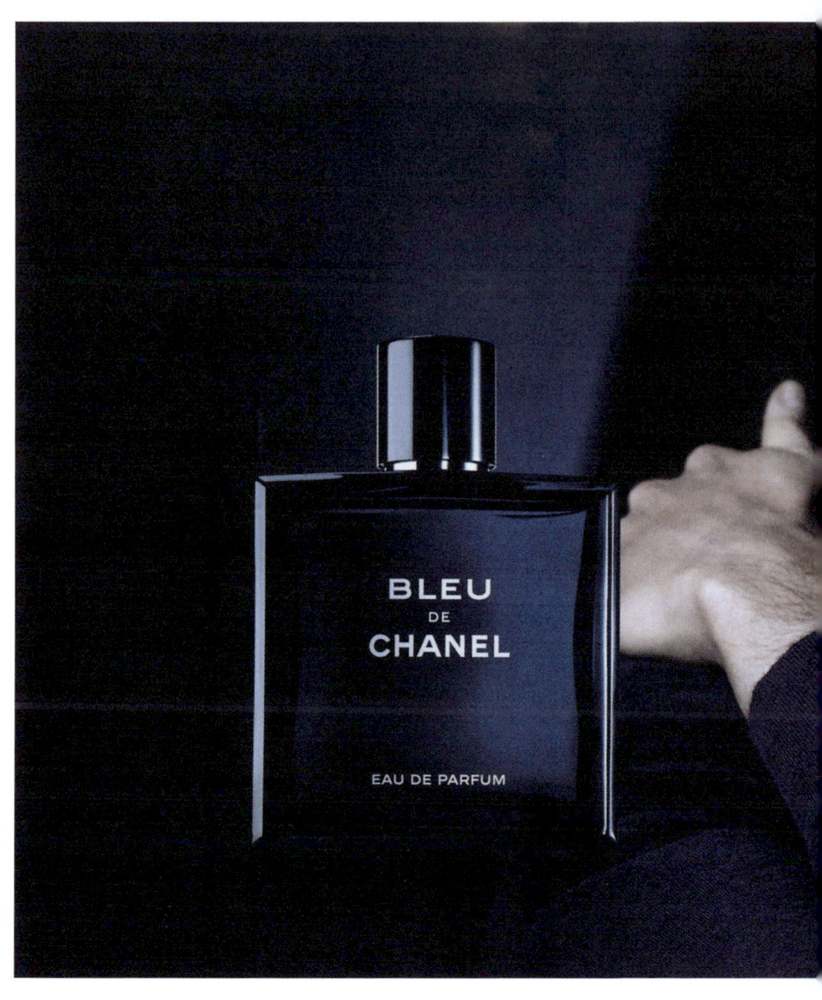

THE TRAGEDY *of* THE BLEU DE CHANEL MODEL

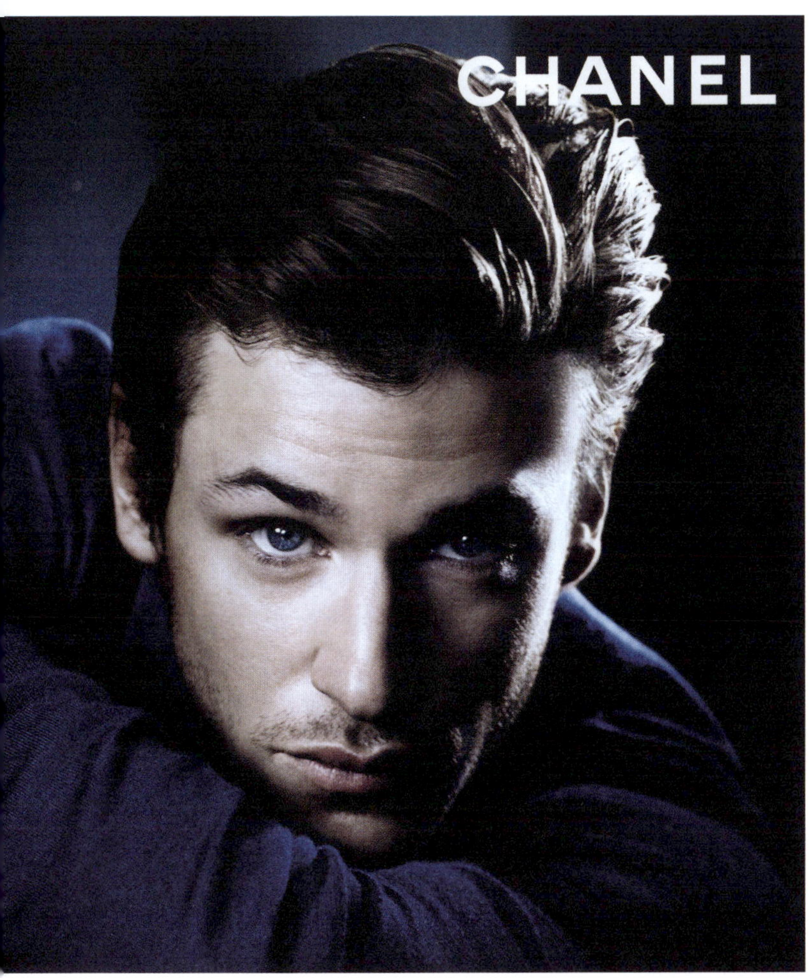

As the face of the Bleu de Chanel fragrance for 12 years, Gaspard Ulliel made quite an impression. He was featured in print ads, television commercials, and mini-films for the popular men's fragrance. As a Paris-based model and actor, he even played Yves Saint Laurent in a 2014 biopic about the designer.

One of the most popular commercials that he did for Bleu de Chanel was in 2010 and was directed by one of the most famous directors in the world, Martin Scorsese. The short film is a gorgeous piece of cinematic art that shows just how handsome and magnetic Gaspard truly was. Sadly, on January 22, 2022, Gaspard died in a skiing accident in France. He was only 37 years old.

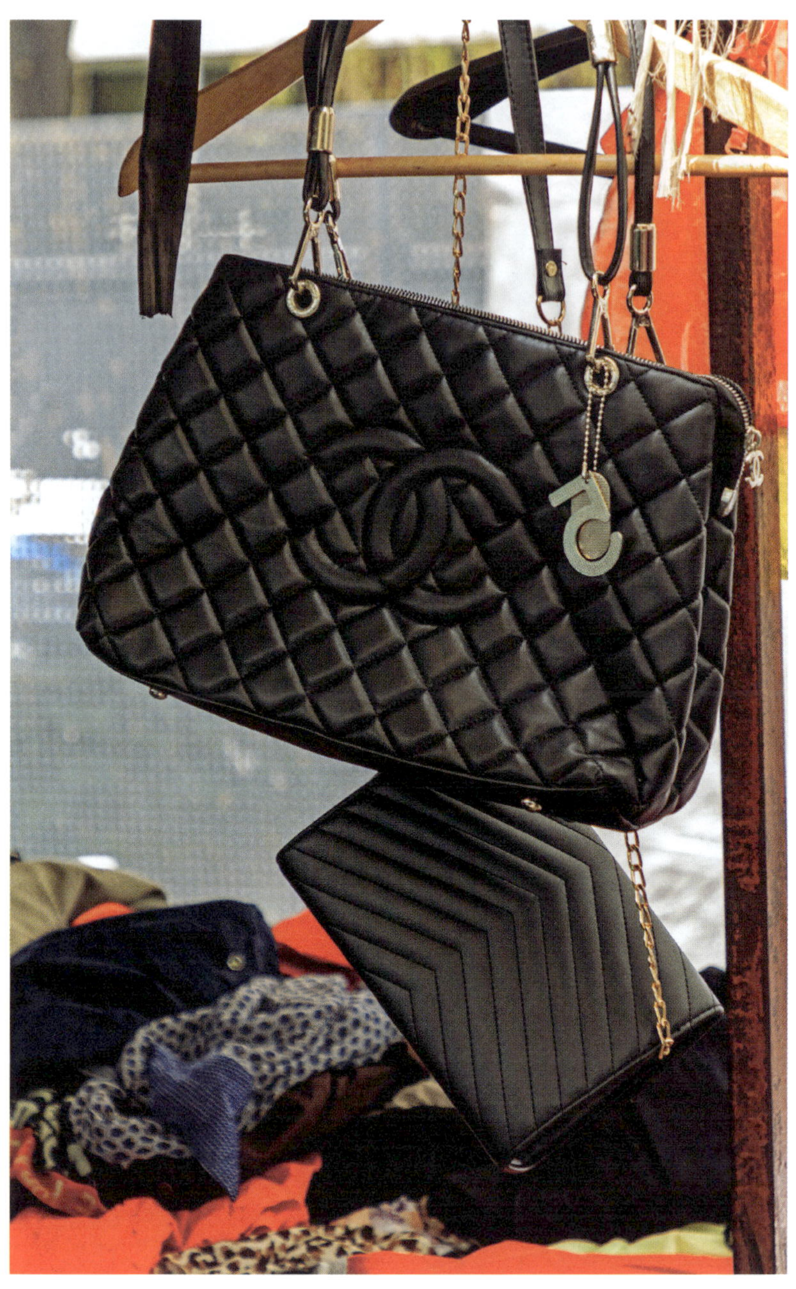

THE WHAT GOES AROUND *Comes* AROUND BATTLE

Chanel was most recently in the headlines in February 2024 for a lawsuit against the luxury resale company What Goes Around Comes Around (WGACA). They were sued by Chanel in 2018 for trademark infringement, false advertising, and selling counterfeit products.

Ultimately, the judge in the case decided in Chanel's favor. WGACA claimed that they always authenticate their products and had never sold anything fake. The judge didn't agree, however, awarding Chanel $4 million in damages. Of course, considering that the House of Chanel brings in approximately $20 billion annually, the fine was primarily symbolic.

Overall, it was a victory for a legacy fashion house against a company that was selling counterfeit products. Chanel is also involved in a current case against another resale website, The RealReal.

"CHANEL IS A LIFESTYLE, AND THERE'S AN *ENERGY* TO IT THAT'S ALIVE."

Pharrell Williams

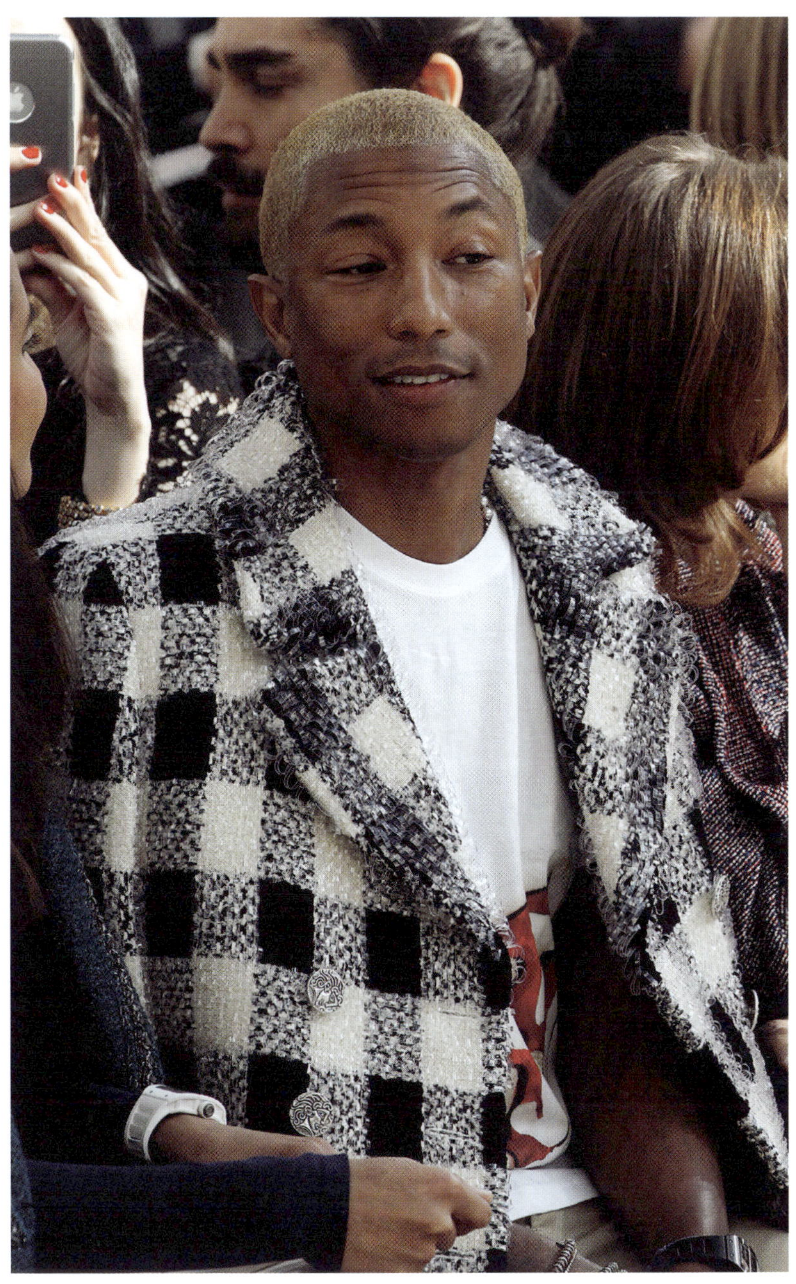

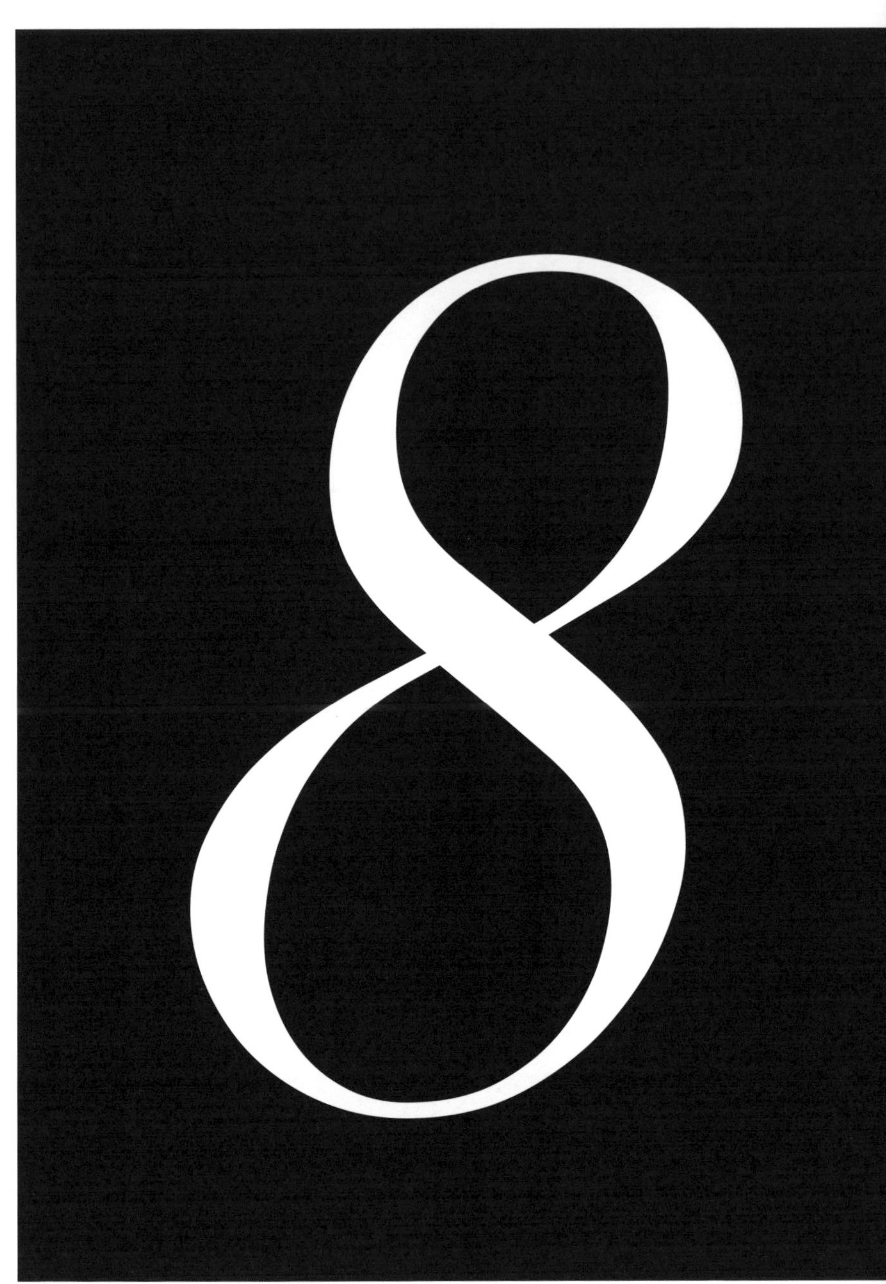

THE FACES *of* CHANEL

Famous Models

TO BE CHOSEN AS A SPOKESPERSON or model for Chanel is a high honor. Over the decades, many famous faces have promoted various lines for the brand. The ads that Chanel creates are legendary, especially the mini-films that act as commercials for the fragrances.

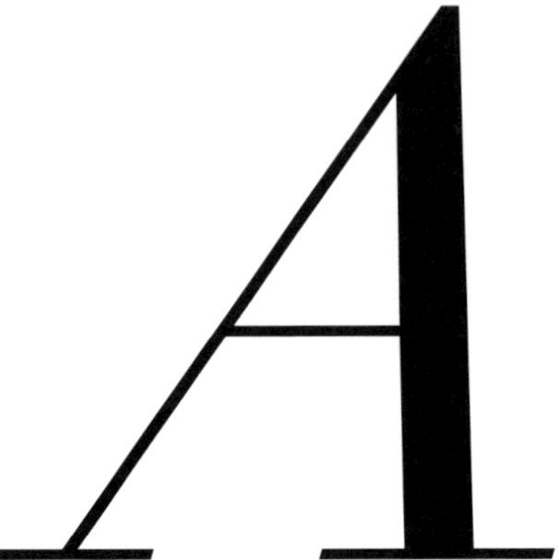

s the creative director for 36 years, Karl Lagerfeld had his favorite models, who he used repeatedly in his spectacular runway shows. He was always personally involved in reaching out to actors and models to be involved with Chanel.

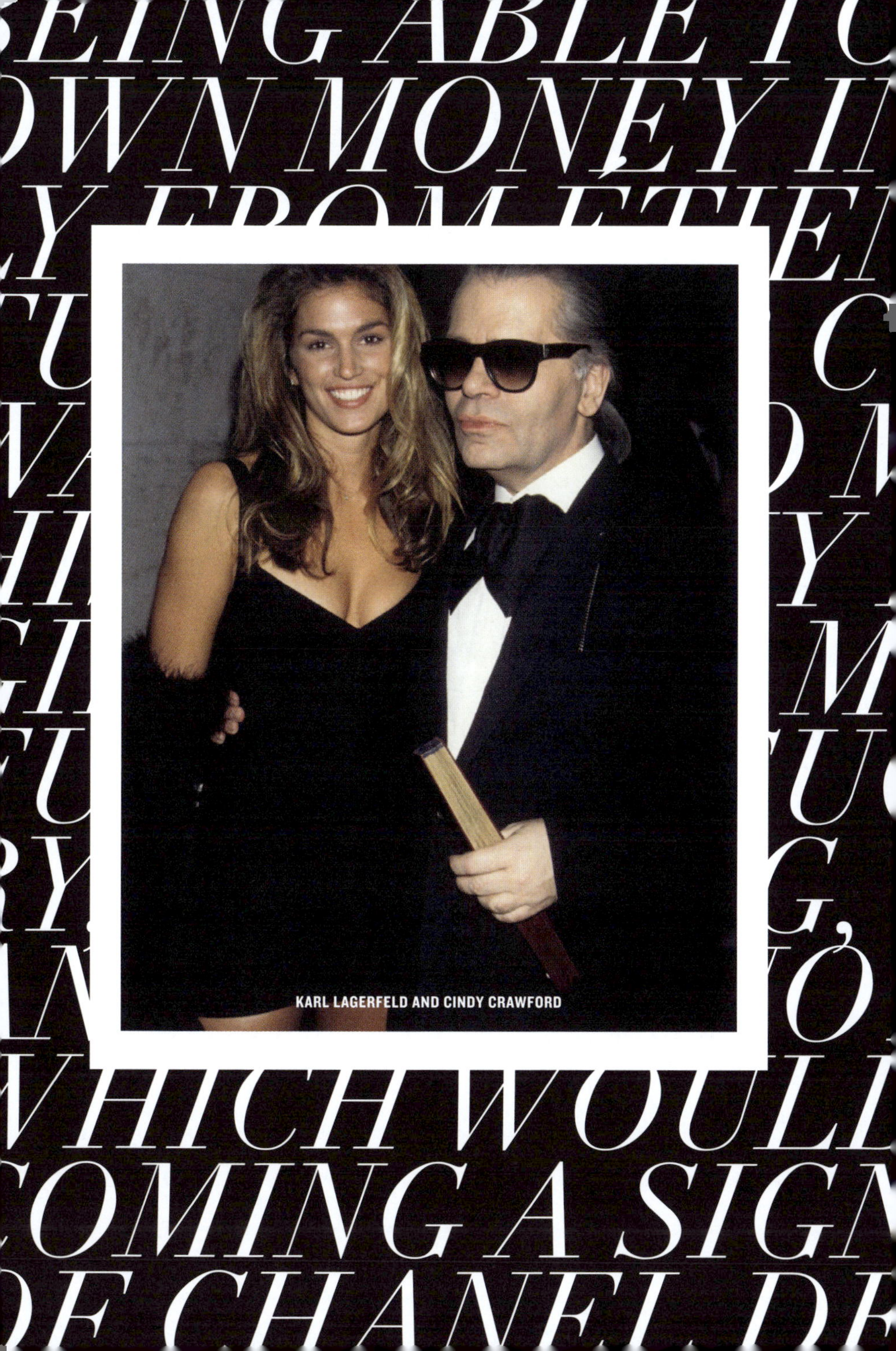

KARL LAGERFELD AND CINDY CRAWFORD

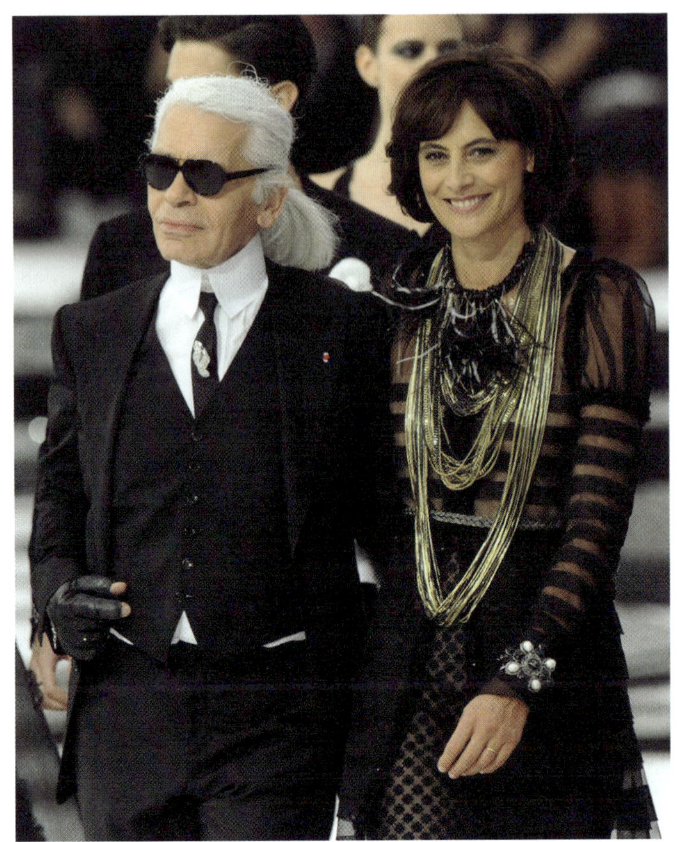

INÈS *de La Fressange*

The first model to sign a long-term contract with Chanel was Inès de La Fressange. Karl signed her to Chanel in 1983 because he thought she resembled Coco Chanel herself—both were beautiful French women. Inès continued her relationship with Chanel until 1989 when she had an argument with Karl over a French political issue. Now 66 years old, she continues to work occasionally as a model and designs her own line.

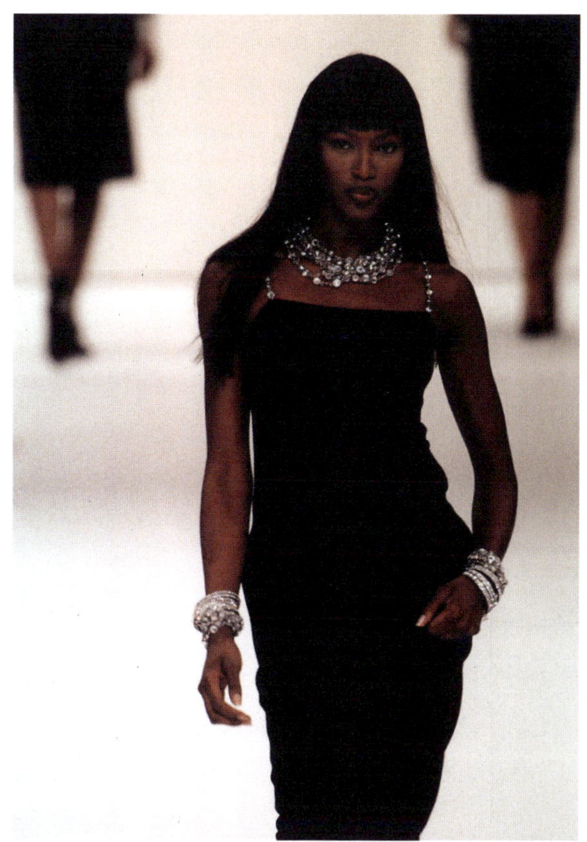

NAOMI *Campbell*

One of Chanel's longest supermodel partnerships has been with Naomi Campbell. She was famously close to Karl and still works for the House of Chanel today at the age of 53. At the 2023 Met Gala honoring Karl, Naomi said that she had many "great memories" working with the fashion genius from when she was 16 years old until he passed away. Her current campaign is for the Spring/Summer 2024 haute couture collection where she is featured in a short ad film called "The Button" alongside actor Margaret Qualley.

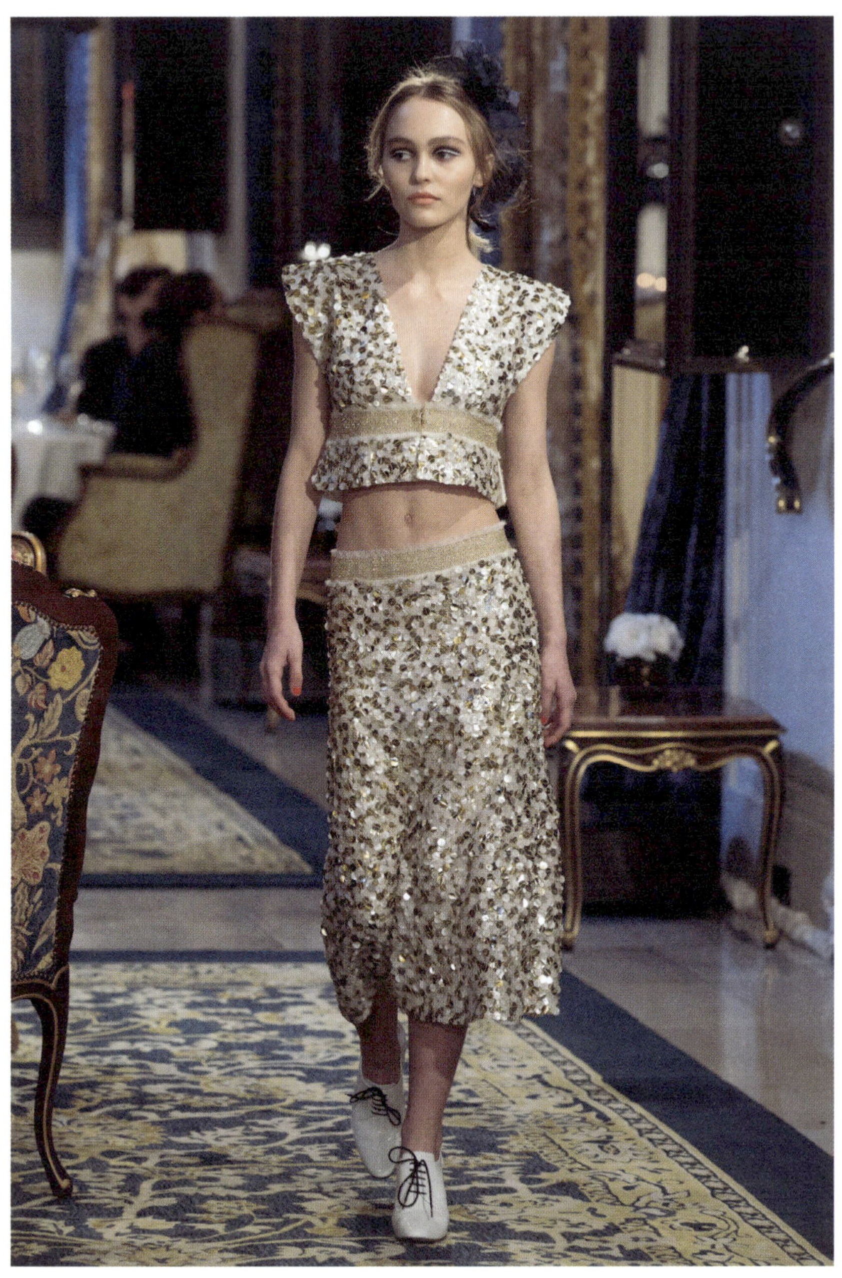

LILY-ROSE
Depp

This actor and model is following in her famous parents' footsteps. Lily-Rose Depp's mother is Vanessa Paradis, who has modeled for Chanel over the years. Her father is Johnny Depp, who has a large fragrance contract with another fashion house, Dior. Lily-Rose has been the face of the Chanel N°5 L'Eau campaign as an ambassador since 2015 and was the youngest ambassador ever when she first modeled the Chanel eyewear collection at just 16.

KRISTEN *Stewart*

Actor Kristen Stewart of the Twilight movies seems like an odd choice for Chanel with her edgy beauty and outspoken nature. Yet, she's been an ambassador for Chanel since 2013, starring in quite a few campaigns and wearing their designs almost exclusively on the red carpet. One of the most famous campaigns that she fronted was for the Gabrielle fragrance. Virginie Viard, current creative director of Chanel, loves to use her because she feels that Kristen embodies the modern Chanel woman.

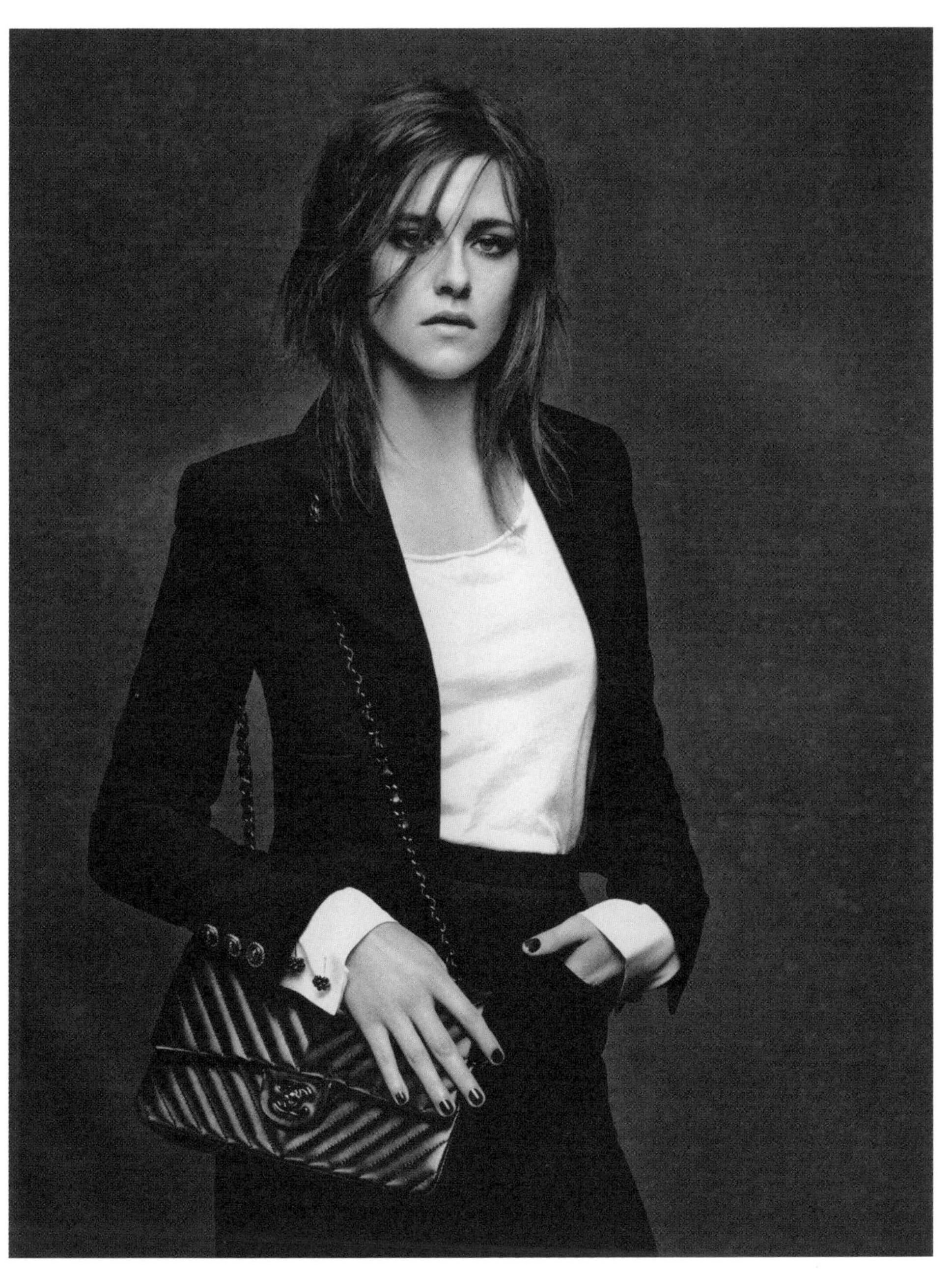

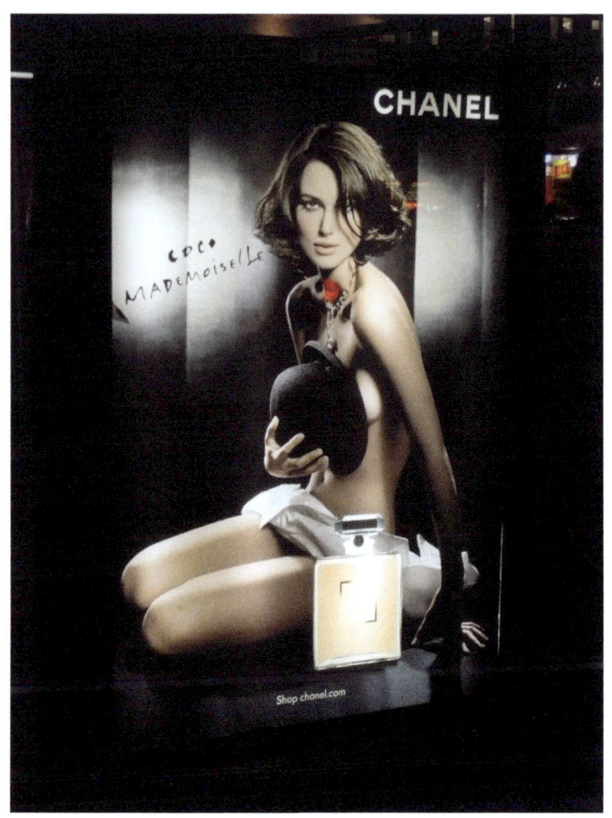

KEIRA *Knightley*

Actor Keira Knightley has been an ambassador for Chanel since 2006. One of the most notable campaigns she does for Chanel is for the fragrance Coco Mademoiselle. Keira is such a fan of Chanel that she even said in an interview that she wore Chanel, including their red lipstick, every day while in lockdown during the pandemic because it was fun for her two little girls. She was very close to Karl and routinely shows up at red-carpet events in Chanel haute couture.

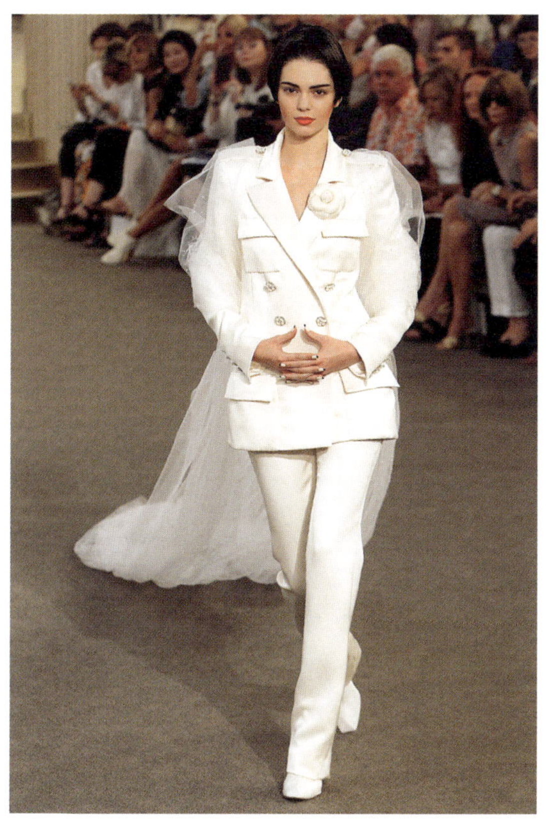

KENDELL *Jenner*

As part of the juggernaut of success that is the Kardashian–Jenner family, Kendall Jenner has made her own way as a supermodel and has been a Chanel ambassador since 2015. One of her most famous campaigns was for the Chanel Gabrielle handbag. She has also walked in quite a few runway shows for the fashion brand, with Karl naming her the face of the Spring/Summer 2015 collection when she was just 19 years old.

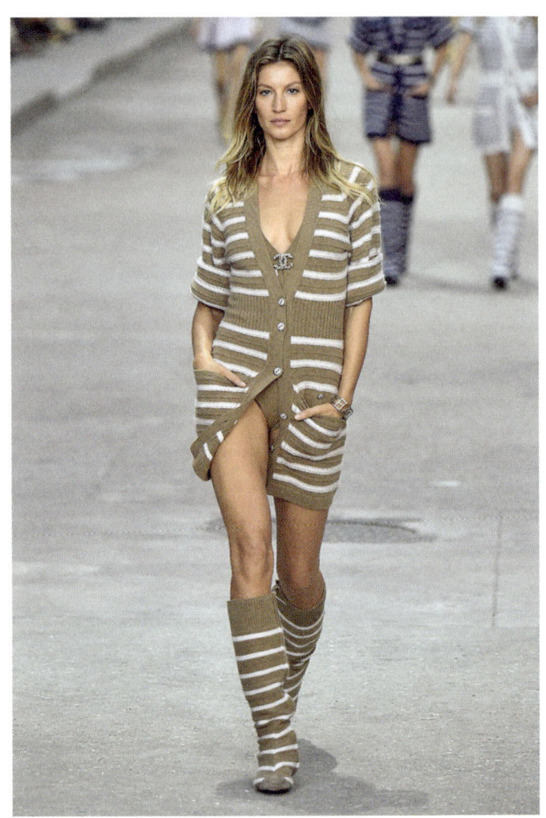

GISELE *Bündchen*

This Brazilian beauty is one of the most famous supermodels in the world. Gisele Bündchen has been with Chanel since 2014 and has been the face of quite a few campaigns, including for Chanel N°5. One of the most famous mini-films she did for Chanel was called "The One That I Want," directed by Baz Luhrmann. In it, she is seen surfing in a Chanel one-piece wetsuit with a Chanel-branded surfboard. It's beyond cool. The ad campaign was meant to display the many sides of a woman who chooses to wear Chanel N°5. Gisele was ideal for this.

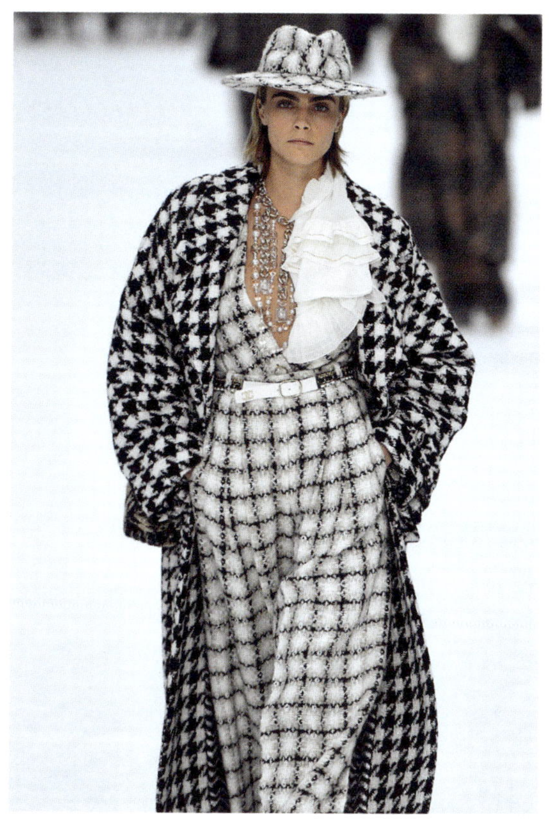

CARA *Delevingne*

Actor and supermodel Cara Delevingne has been seen on the Chanel runway multiple times and featured in quite a few ad campaigns. She first walked the Chanel runway in 2012 when Karl personally chose her. Cara has often said that Karl changed her life when he picked her that day. She even gave a speech at his memorial service in 2019.

PHARRELL *Williams*

Pharrell Williams is truly a renaissance man. As a musician, producer, and fashion designer, he has had a long relationship with Chanel, which began in 2014. He is the first man to produce a capsule collection with the brand. One of those pieces was a faux crocodile tote bag in 2018 that he was seen with during Paris Fashion Week. Pharrell was featured in the Spring 2020 eyewear campaign with a pair of oversized logo sunglasses that are classic Chanel.

MARGOT *Robbie*

Margot Robbie has been an ambassador for Chanel since 2018, though there is some controversy about her involvement with the label. She is often seen on the red carpet in Chanel clothing, but some say that she isn't happy about it because she doesn't actually like the designs. Luckily for Margot, her contract ended in 2022 and she has been able to make different choices about what she wears since then, including during the press tour for Barbie, which was a billion-dollar success.

TIMOTHÉE *Chalamet*

Timothée Chalamet is one of the hottest actors of his generation. His involvement with Chanel began when he became the new ambassador for the Bleu de Chanel men's fragrance. Already he has shot multiple film and print campaigns for the brand since 2023. His boyish good looks, winning charm, and subtle smile are going to entice a whole new generation of Chanel fans.

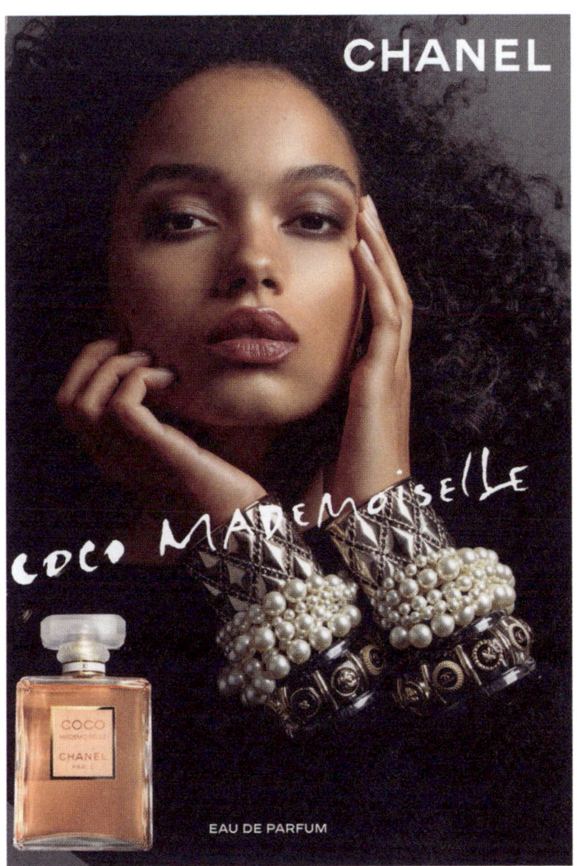

WHITNEY *Peak*

Another young actor who is luring the next generation of Chanel lovers is Whitney Peak. She recently starred in the reboot of "Gossip Girl" and at 21 years old is one of the newest "it girls." In 2023, Whitney was chosen to be the new face of Coco Mademoiselle. This was significant, not only because she started as a brand ambassador for the Chanel 22 handbag campaign but because she is making history as the first African American face of Chanel.

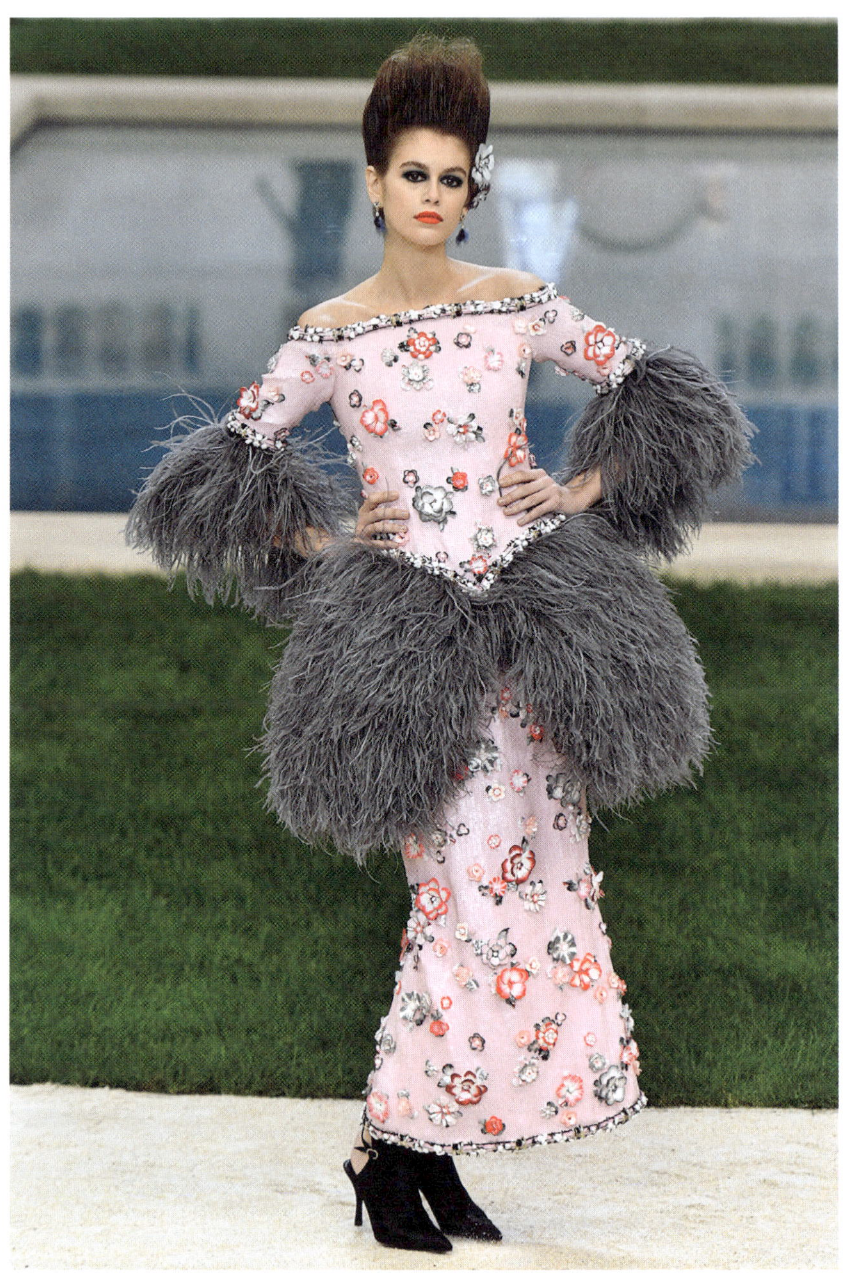

“CHANEL IS MORE THAN JUST A FASHION HOUSE; *IT'S A SYMBOL OF GRACE, STRENGTH, AND TIMELESS BEAUTY. IT'S AN HONOR TO BE ASSOCIATED WITH A BRAND THAT REPRESENTS SUCH ICONIC ELEGANCE.*”

Kaia Gerber

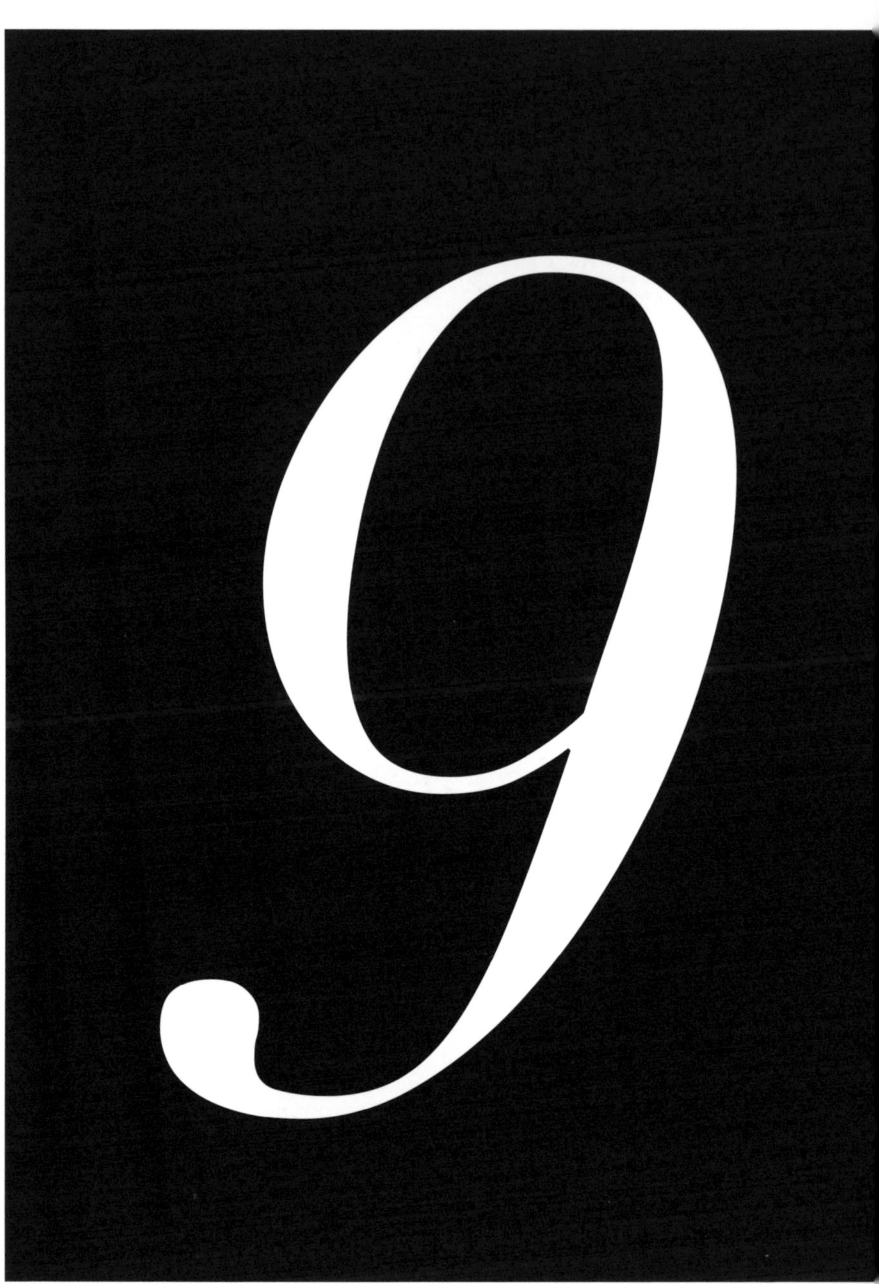

CHANEL *on all* THE STARS

Celebrities

CHANEL HAS A VERY PRESTIGIOUS HISTORY. Because of this, many celebrities are more than willing to wear Chanel haute couture on the red carpet for award shows and other important events. Both men and women look fabulous in classic Chanel, a timeless brand that has dressed movie stars, musicians, politicians, and royalty since the 1930s. Here are some of the most memorable looks by the House of Chanel to appear on the famous and fabulous over the decades.

PRINCESS *DIANA*

The lovely Princess Diana of Wales wore the classic Chanel suit on many occasions. She wore one of her best versions of the suit while attending the confirmation of her son, Prince William, in 1997 at Windsor Castle. It was a baby blue wool Chanel suit with a matching pillbox hat, light fringe around the edges, and Chanel logo buttons. She paired the look with a beige handbag and nude pumps. All in all, it was a memorable look for a very important occasion for the future king of England. Sadly, this was one of the last looks she was seen in publicly because just a few months later she died in a tragic car accident.

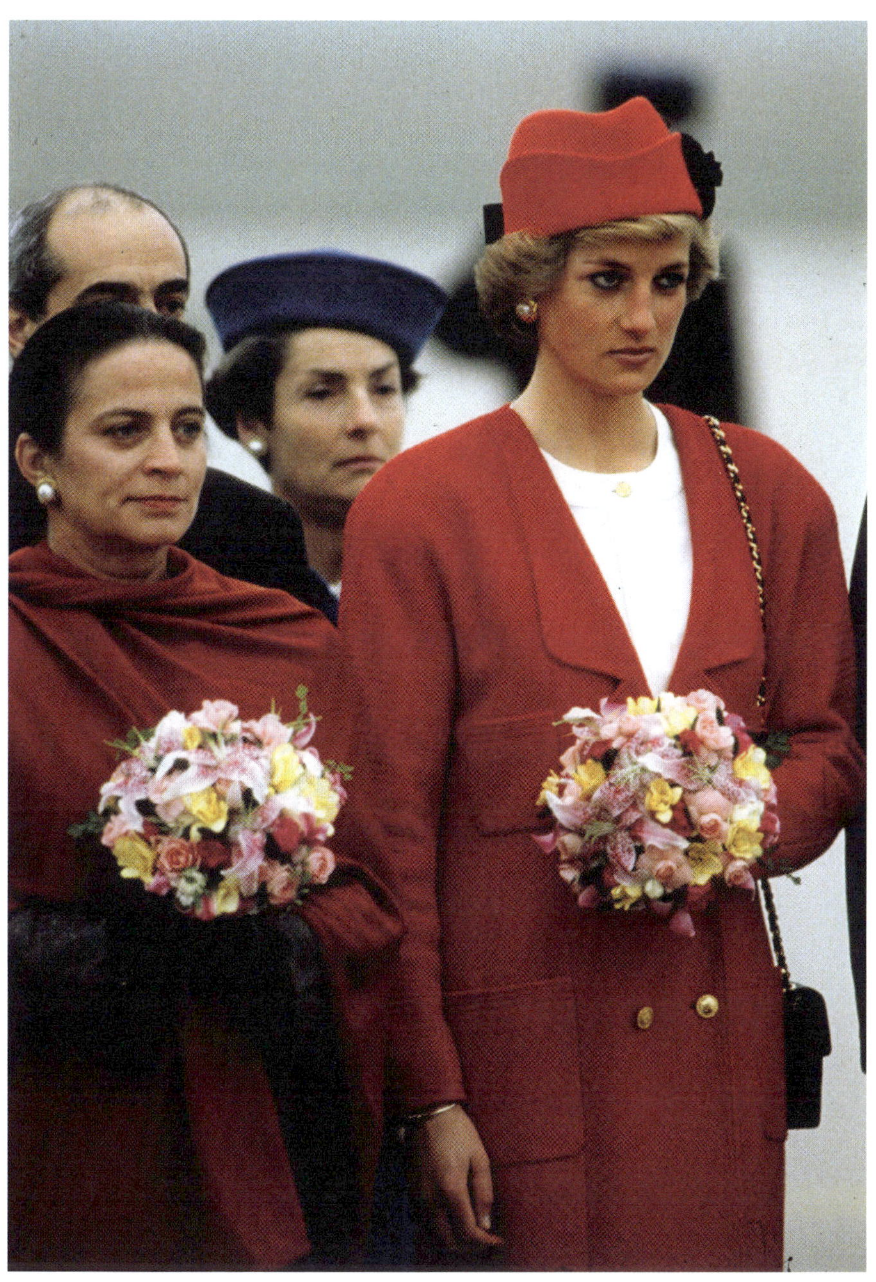

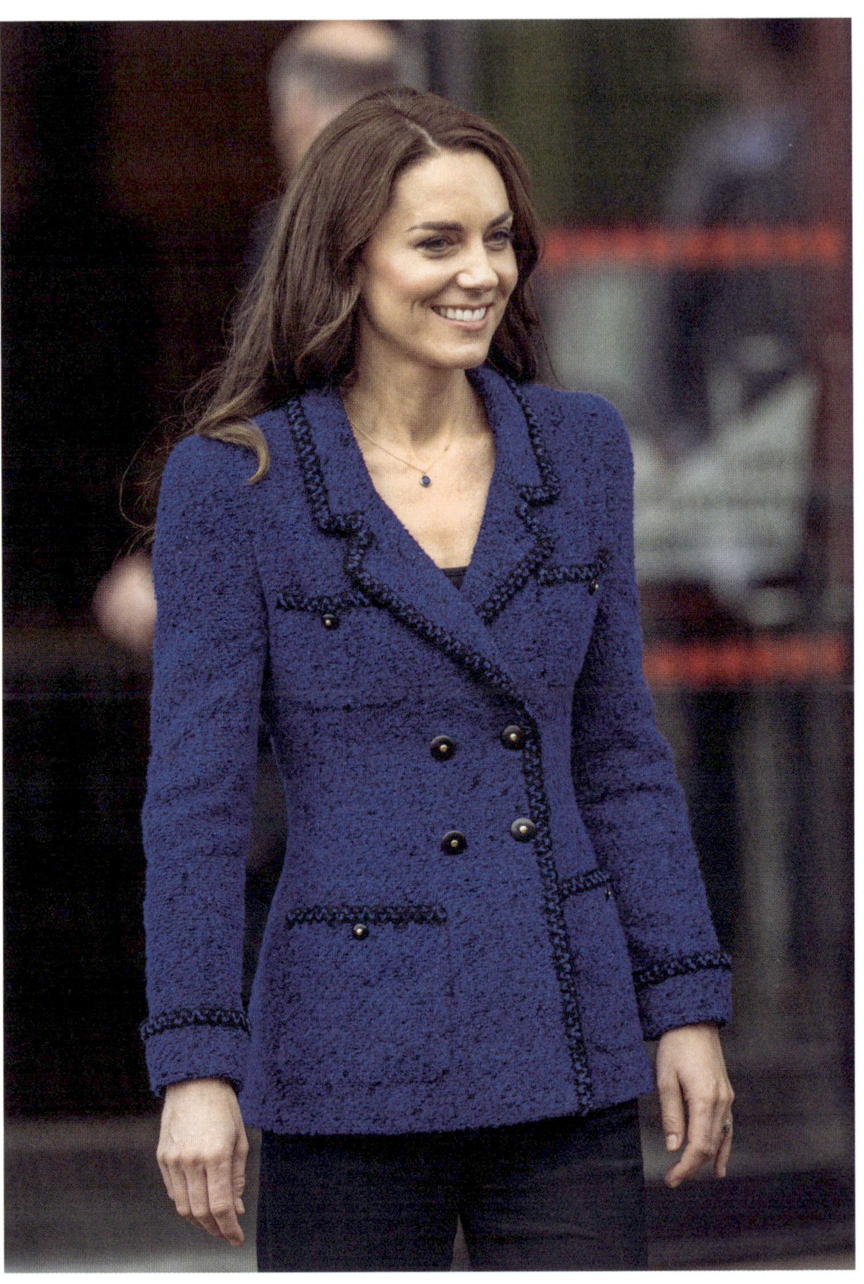

PRINCESS *KATE*

Princess Kate has followed in her mother-in-law's footsteps, wearing classic Chanel suits to various events over the years. Several different Chanel handbags are also part of her regular rotation. Some of the most famous looks that Princess Kate has worn were on a trip to Paris with her husband as part of their royal duties. Karl Lagerfeld personally chose her wardrobe for the trip with one of the best looks being a tweed blazer dress with a flared skirt and a Chanel logo belt. It had a knee-length hemline and fitted waist, and the princess carried a burgundy quilted leather top-handled Chanel bag. The whole look was a modern take on the Chanel suit that the press went wild for.

BLAKE *LIVELY*

Actor Blake Lively is a good friend to Chanel. Over the years, she has been photographed many times on the red carpet in gorgeous Chanel couture. One of the most exquisite dresses she wore was in 2011 at the Met Gala. It was a Chanel couture, Greek-inspired goddess gown with taupe draping over a silver embroidered nude bodice from the 2009 collection. Since she was close with Karl, there are pictures of them together at this posh event.

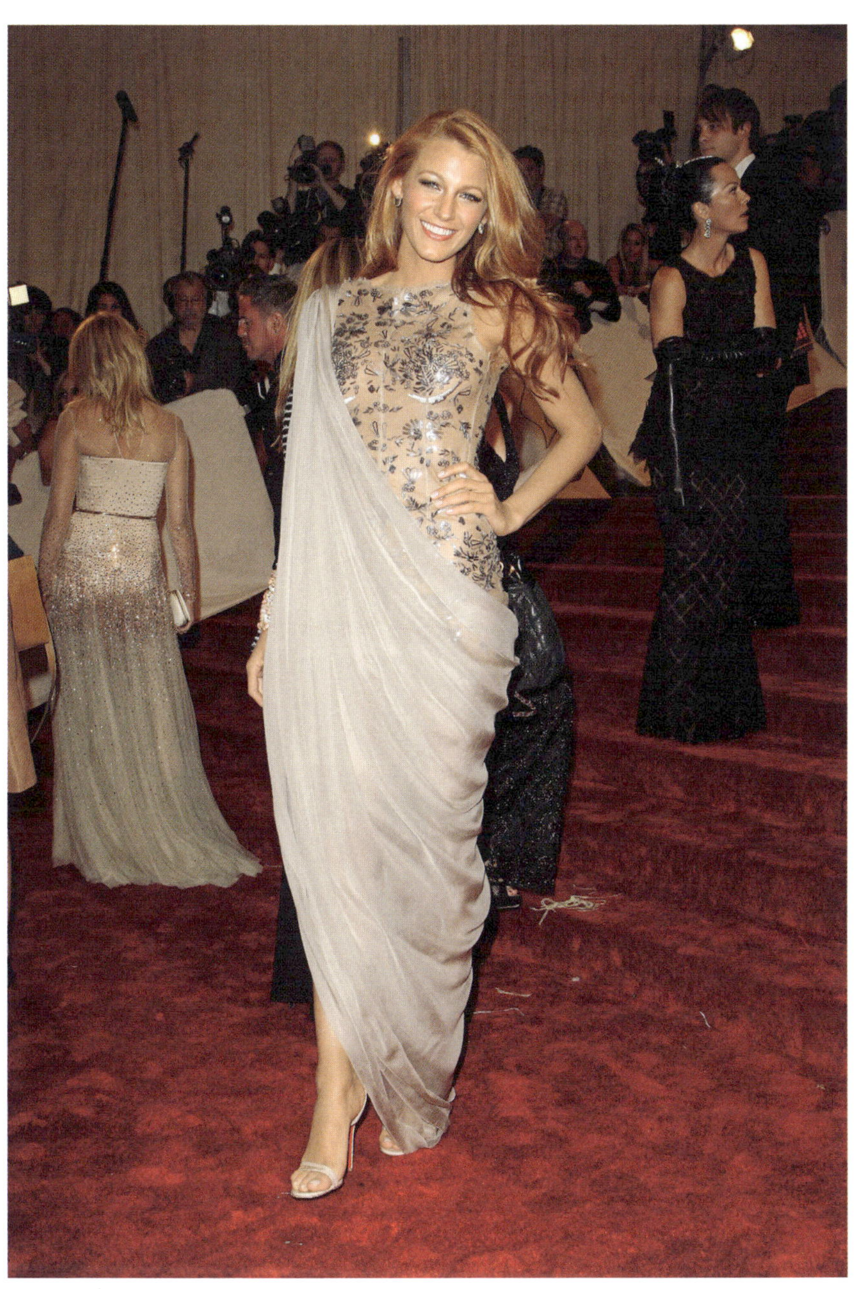

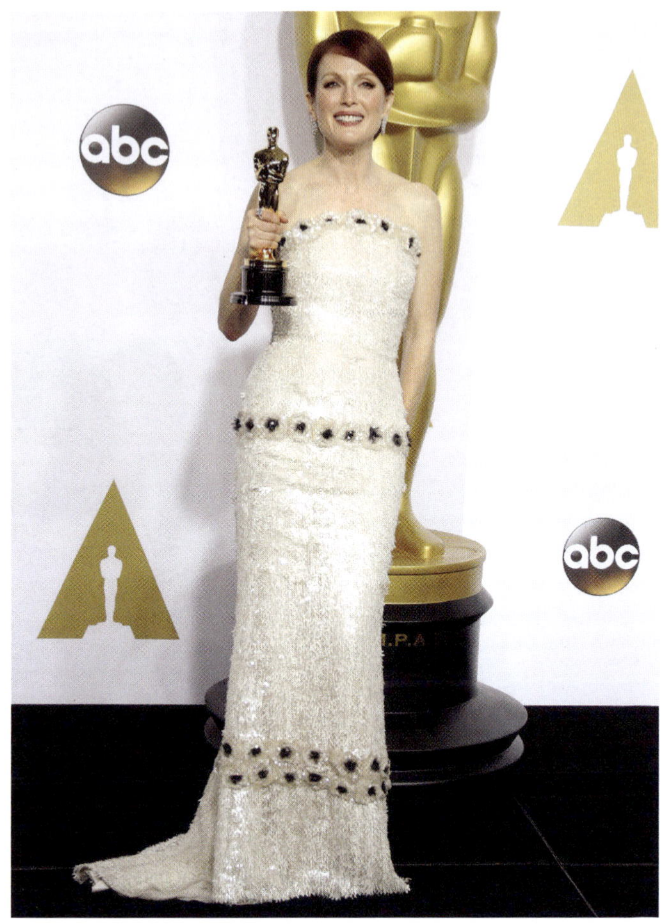

JULIANNE *MOORE*

Red-haired beauty and actor Julianne Moore looks like she's from another era each time she wears Chanel. Her 2015 Academy Awards dress was a showstopper. It was a one-of-a-kind creation from Chanel designed by Karl Lagerfeld himself. A strapless gown in white organza with a hidden bustier and silk underlay, it had a whopping 80,000 hand-painted resin sequins in the shape of flower patterns, which made this dress quite unique. The House of Chanel estimated that it took dressmakers almost 1,000 hours to create this masterpiece. It must have been a lucky dress, too, as Julianne ended up winning an Oscar that night.

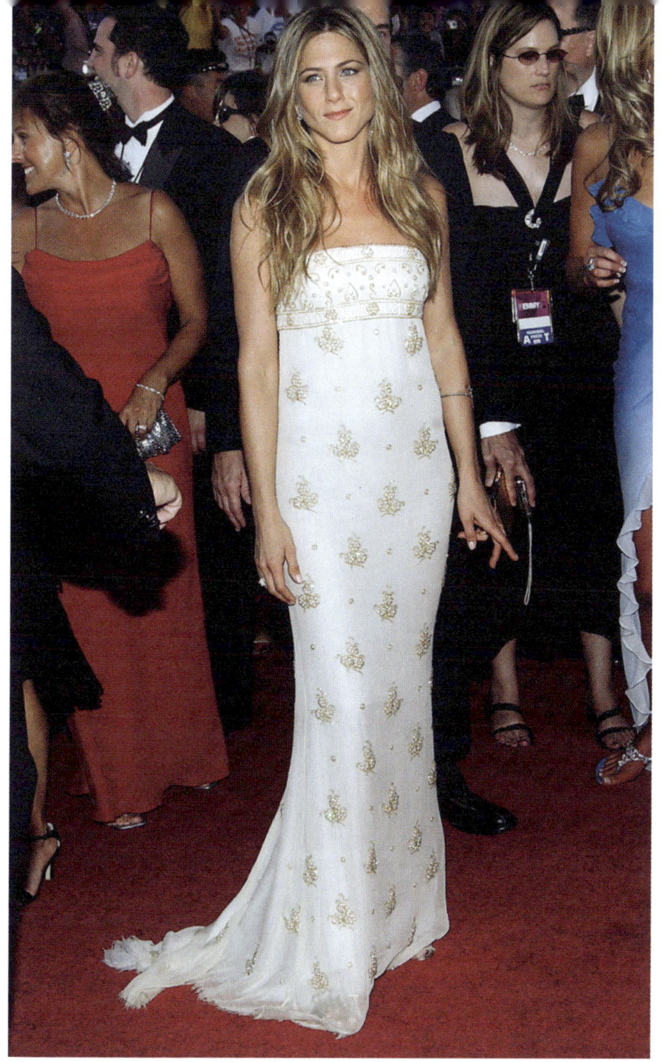

JENNIFER *ANISTON*

Our favorite "Friend" is always a red-carpet standout. The looks that she has worn over the years from Chanel are stunning. One very tiny yet memorable look was featured on the cover of Allure in 2022. It was an itty-bitty, vintage 1996 Chanel micro-bikini top that had logos right in the center of each side. On the red carpet, she's worn more modest styles, including a Chanel Grecian strapless ivory dress with gold detailing at the 2004 Emmy Awards. She looked like an absolute goddess.

PENELOPE *CRUZ*

Spanish actor Penelope Cruz was a longtime friend of Karl. Her relationship continues with the House of Chanel today, and one of the most recent gowns that she wore was to the Venice Film Festival in 2021. This black and white dress took 300 hours to make and was called "Look Number 34" for the Fall/Winter 2022 collection. With a long, full skirt, petal-shaped ruffles on the sides, and a sheer cream-colored tulle petticoat underneath, this was a magnificent and memorable piece of fashion art.

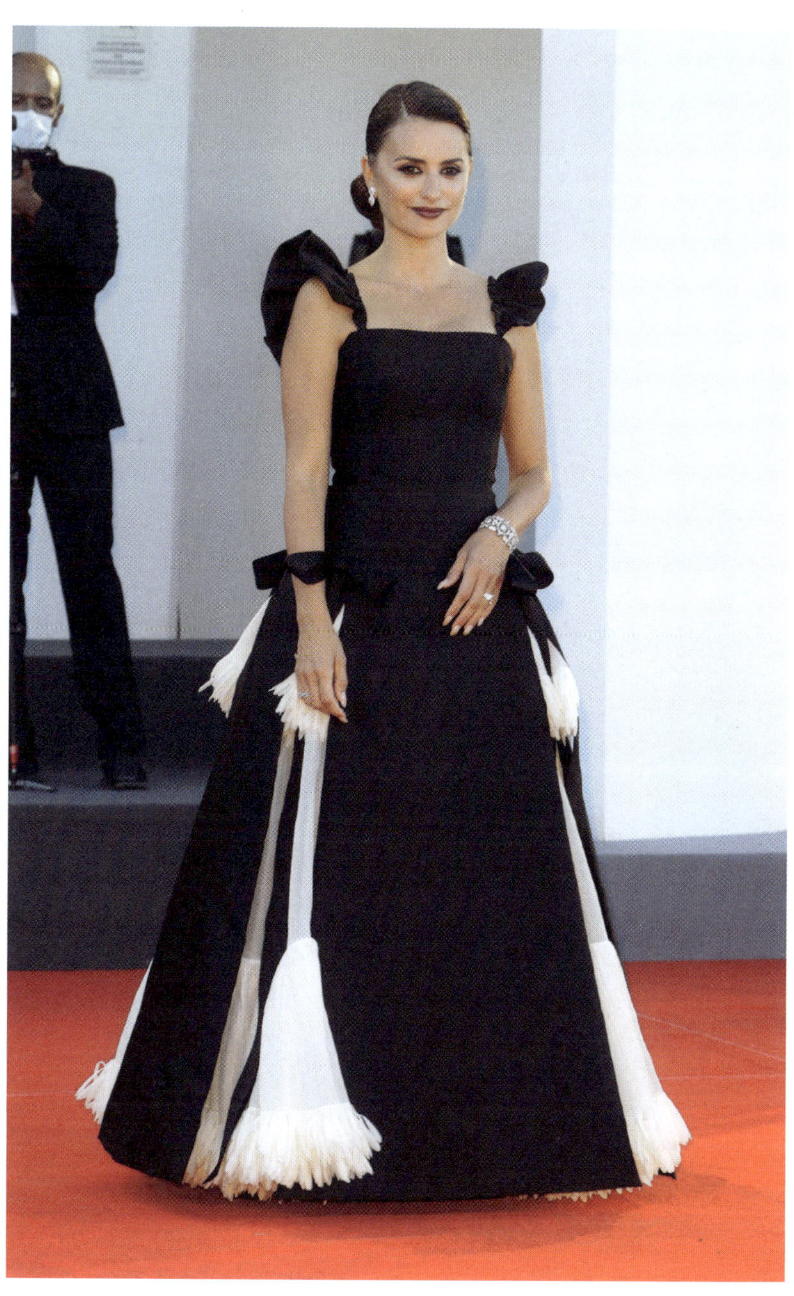

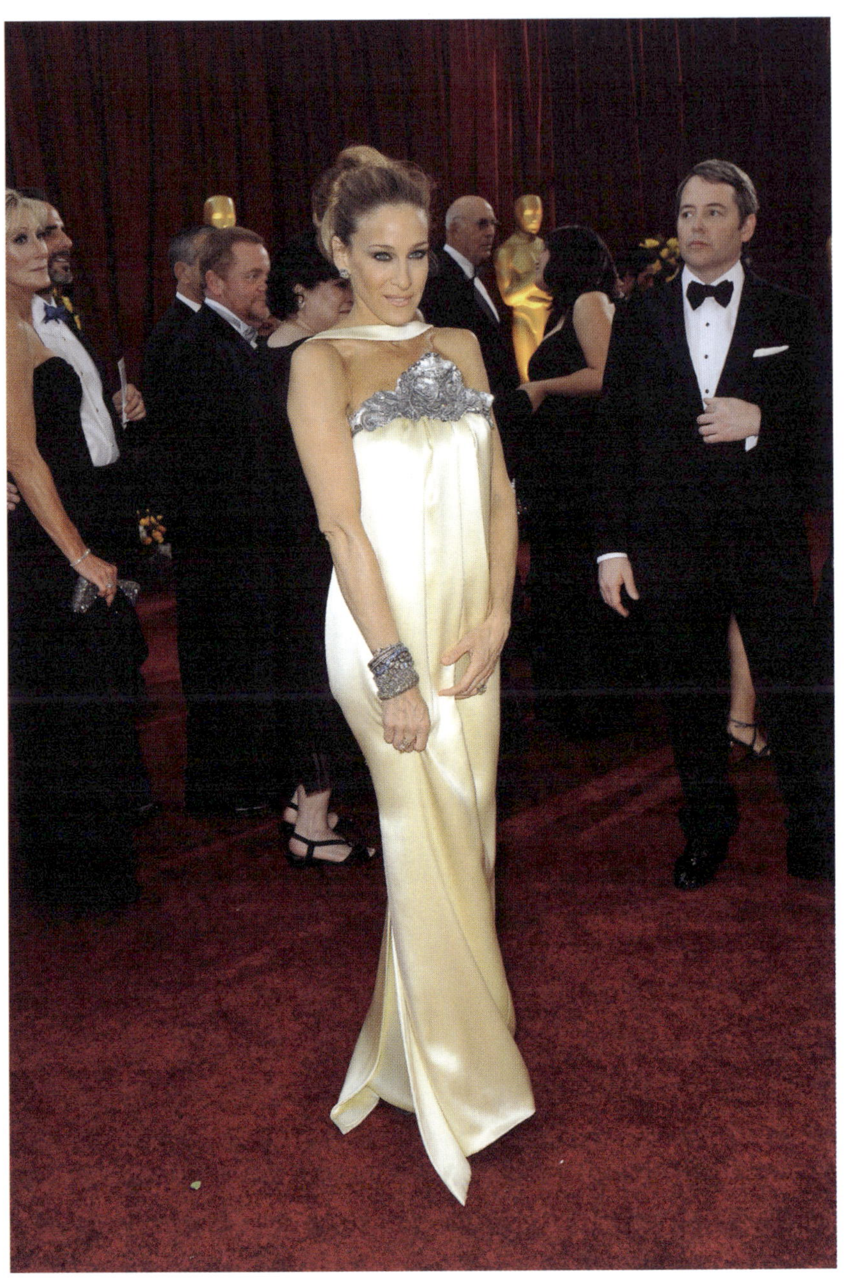

SARAH *JESSICA PARKER*

Actor and fashionista Sarah Jessica Parker is well known for wearing Chanel. Her 2010 Academy Awards dress was a strapless, cream-colored silk creation with a choker of the same material. At the top of the dress around the decolletage were silver fabric roses that trailed down the back of the low-cut dress. Though some of the press thought that the dress was a bit frumpy and shapeless in photos, in person it came across much better.

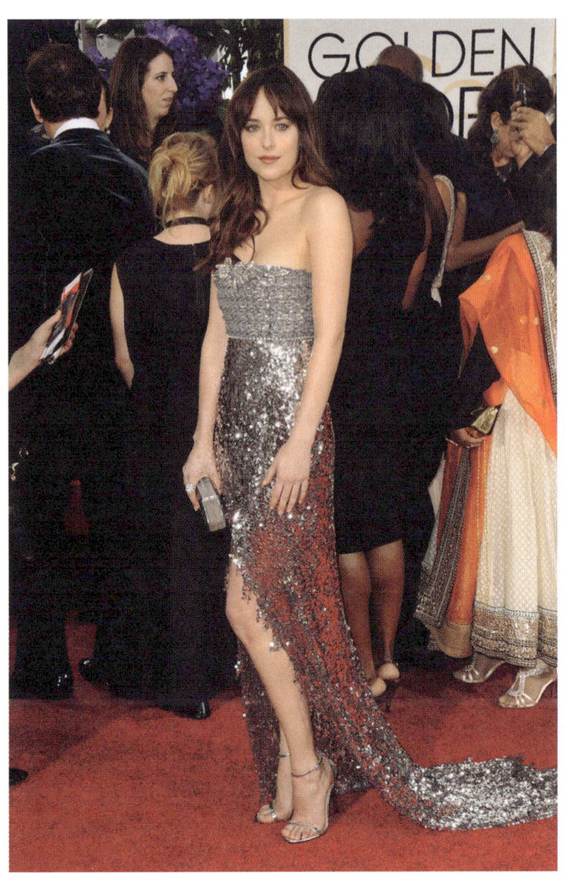

DAKOTA *JOHNSON*

Fifty Shades of Grey actor Dakota Johnson always shines on the red carpet. Coming from an entertainment family, she is well-versed in wearing lovely clothes and couture. For the 2015 Golden Globes, she was photographed in a strapless Chanel creation with silver sequins and shimmering details all the way down the train. The House of Chanel even held this dress for her and didn't let any other stars wear it ahead of the Hollywood event.

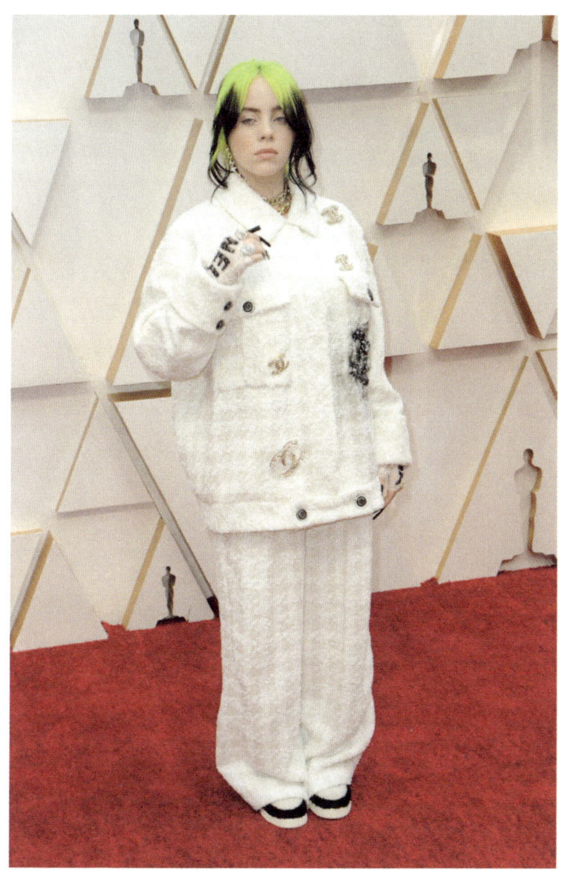

BILLIE *EILISH*

A singer with an interesting sense of style, Billie Eilish showed up on the 2020 Academy Awards red carpet in a baggy, cream-colored Chanel suit. Fluffy, oversized tweed with matching pants, the suit featured crystal brooches with the Chanel logo. Her white lace gloves had Chanel spelled out in black for a unique look that turned heads. The earrings and gold chains that she wore were also Chanel. In 2024, Billie Eilish again showed up for the Academy Awards in Chanel. This time it was a more classic Chanel suit with a structured black blazer and a tweed pencil skirt. She won an Oscar for the song that she did for the Barbie movie, "What Was I Made For?" Clearly, Billie was made to wear Chanel.

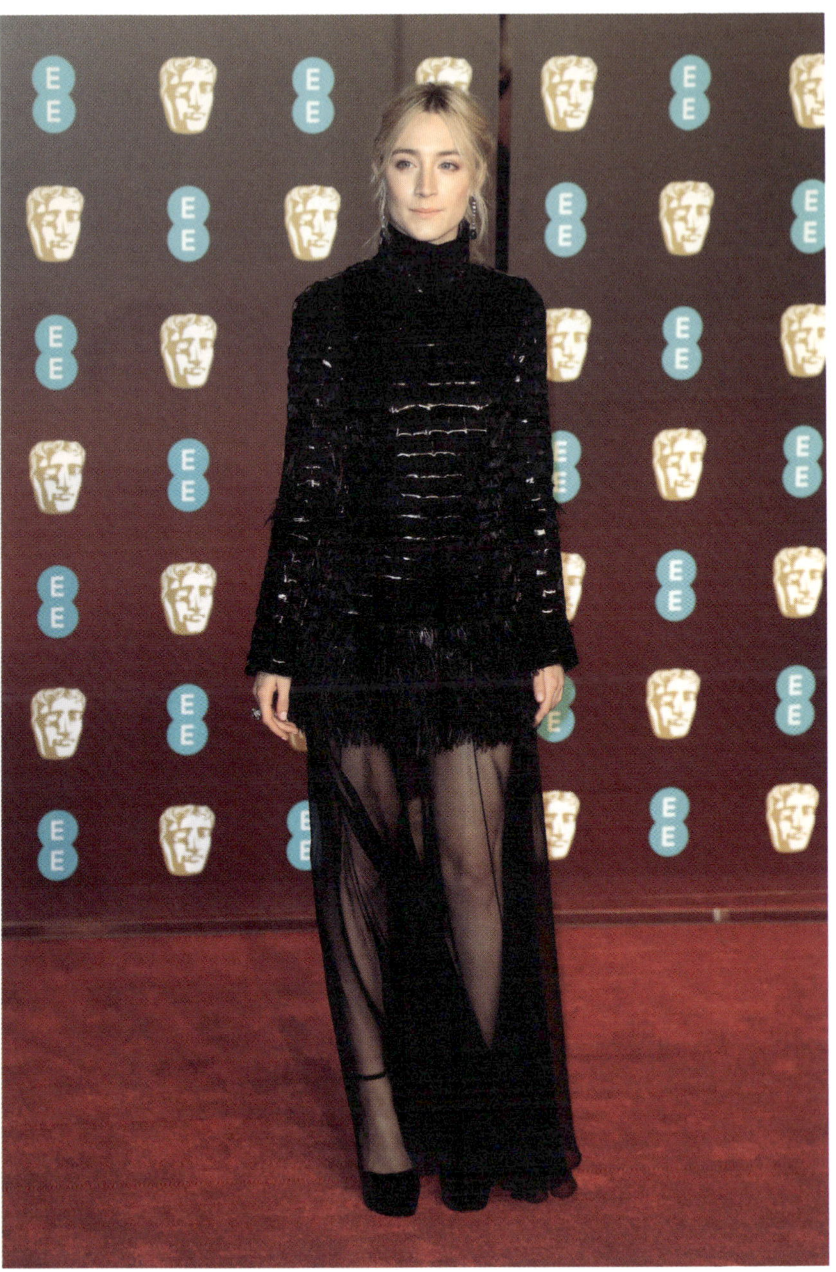
EE

"CHANEL HAS THIS MAGICAL ABILITY TO MAKE YOU FEEL SIMULTANEOUSLY CLASSIC AND MODERN. IT'S LIKE STEPPING INTO A WORLD WHERE ELEGANCE NEVER GOES OUT OF STYLE."

Saoirse Ronan

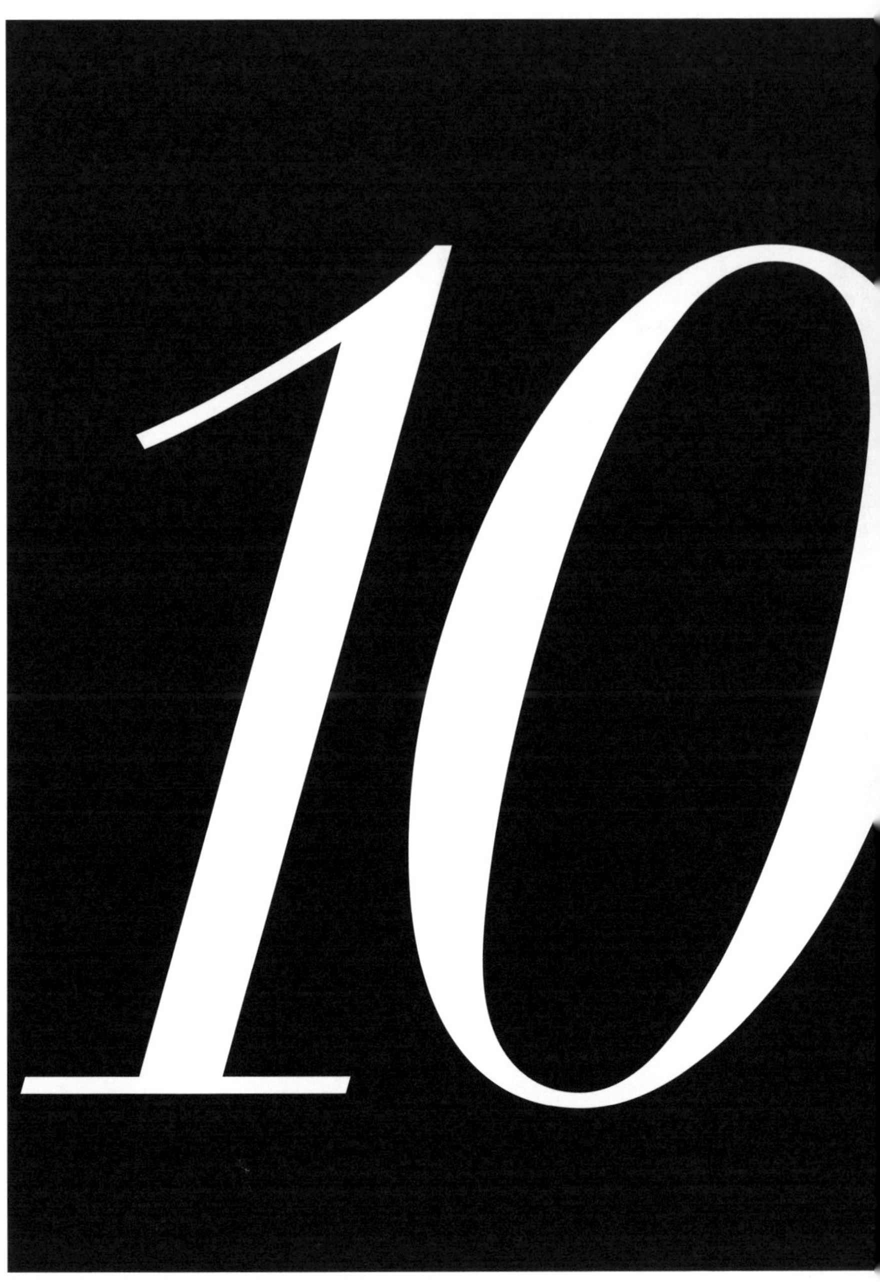
10

CHANEL *for* THE NEW GENERATION

The Future

CHANEL IS A FASHION HOUSE that has been around for 114 years. Chanel's global CEO, Leena Nair, was interviewed in 2023 at a fashion conference about her thoughts on the future of house.

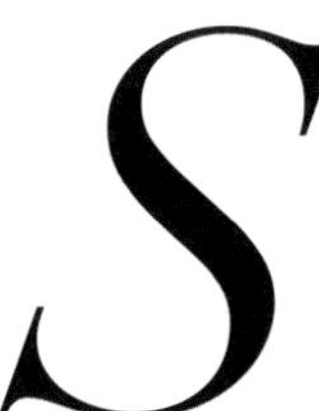

he was hired by the brand two years ago. Other key people currently at Chanel are the creative director, Virginie Viard, the CFO Philippe Blondiaux, and Olivier Polge, head perfumer. The company is privately owned by the billionaire Wertheimer family, who have been involved with the fashion house since making a deal with Coco Chanel in 1924.

When Leena Nair was interviewed, she stated that the three pillars for Chanel in the future were the following: "One is to have a positive impact in the world. ... The second is, in the world of AI, to be relentless in protecting human creation, human creators, and human relationships. And third, to always be part of what's next to shape what's coming."

Chanel and the Climate

Chanel is committed to sustainability and climate action. They are championing the Chanel Mission 1.5, a climate plan through 2030. The mission is to use science-based initiatives to reduce their carbon footprint across all factors of operations, including the supply chain. They are working with the standards created by the Paris Agreement on Climate Change (COP21). Chanel wants a 50 percent reduction in carbon emissions by 2030, as well as a 40 percent reduction in emissions from their supply chain. Additionally, they want to shift to 100 percent renewable electricity in their operations by 2025. These are achievable and definitive goals that hopefully Chanel will be able to accomplish by the target dates.

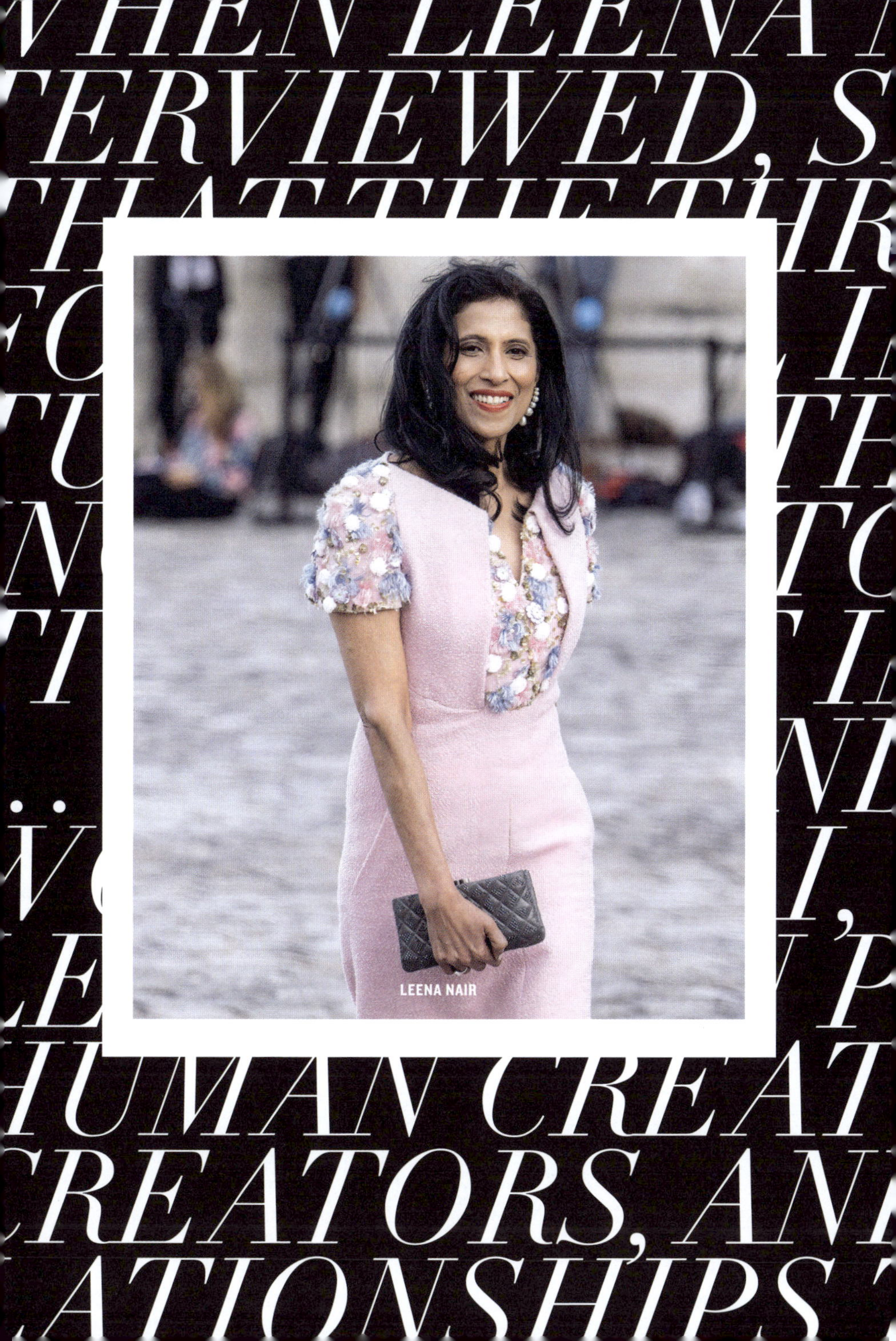

LEENA NAIR

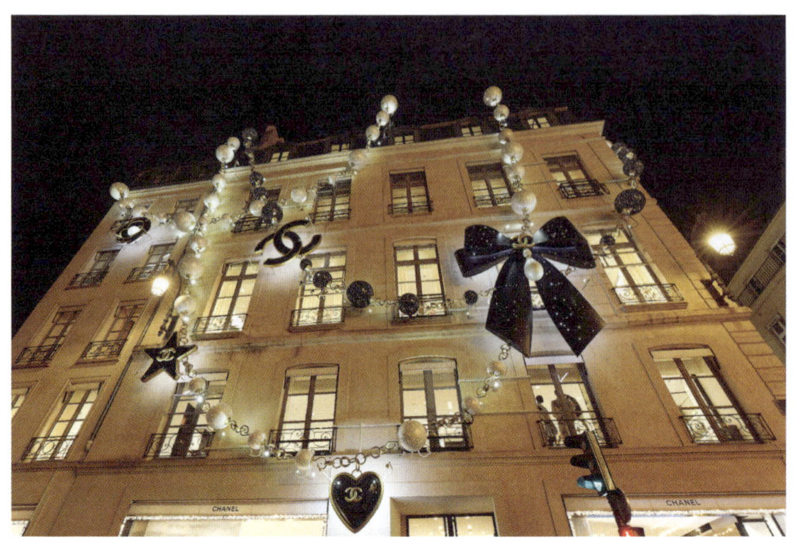
CHANEL
CHANEL

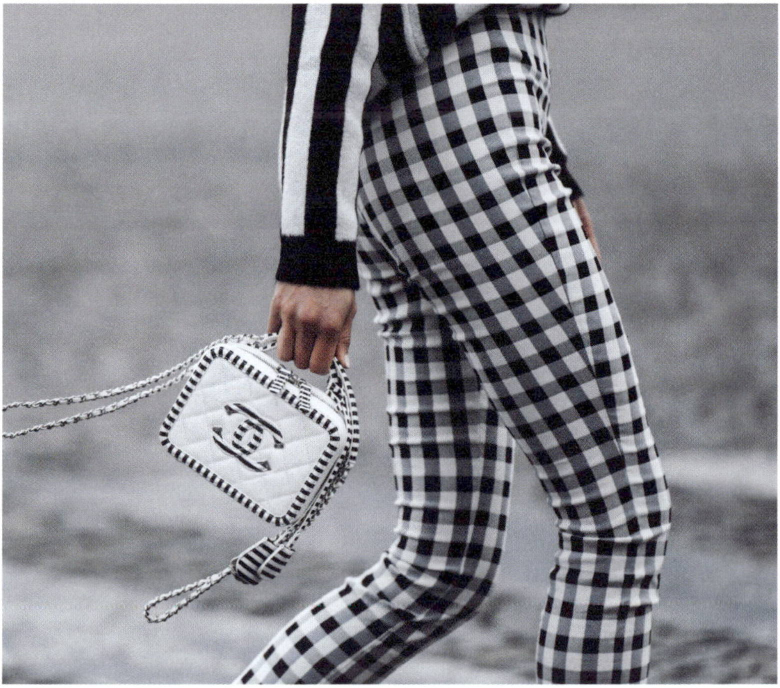

In looking at innovative products from Chanel, they've recently created their first beauty product line that is entirely eco-design driven. It's called N°1 de Chanel, a skincare line that uses 97 percent natural origin ingredients. Each part of the product's lifecycle is meant to reduce its carbon footprint, and the ingredients are farmed using more environmentally friendly practices. Plus, the packaging design of this skincare line is more eco-friendly, using fewer materials in its creation. Even the promotional in-store material advertising the line is made from recycled sources. It's a thoughtful launch and one that will influence the rest of the beauty world in the years to come.

Foundation Chanel

This nonprofit charitable endeavor was created in 2011. The goal of the foundation is for "women and girls to be free to shape their own destiny." It's a cause that Coco Chanel championed in her life and through her work in creating the House of Chanel.

The foundation partners with other nonprofits around the world to help women and girls find economic and educational opportunities in a variety of areas. They are currently working on 65 projects in 35 different countries.

Heading Into the New Era

Chanel is truly and always has been at the forefront of fashion in everything they do. They even have a podcast that has been going on for three seasons now called Chanel Connects. It's eight episodes a week that feature global thought leaders, artists, creators, actors, and musicians who are having an impact on the world today. As an award-winning arts and culture podcast, this is one of the modern ways Chanel is connecting with the future and new generations who love the brand.

"FASHION FADES; ONLY STYLE REMAINS THE SAME."

Coco Chanel

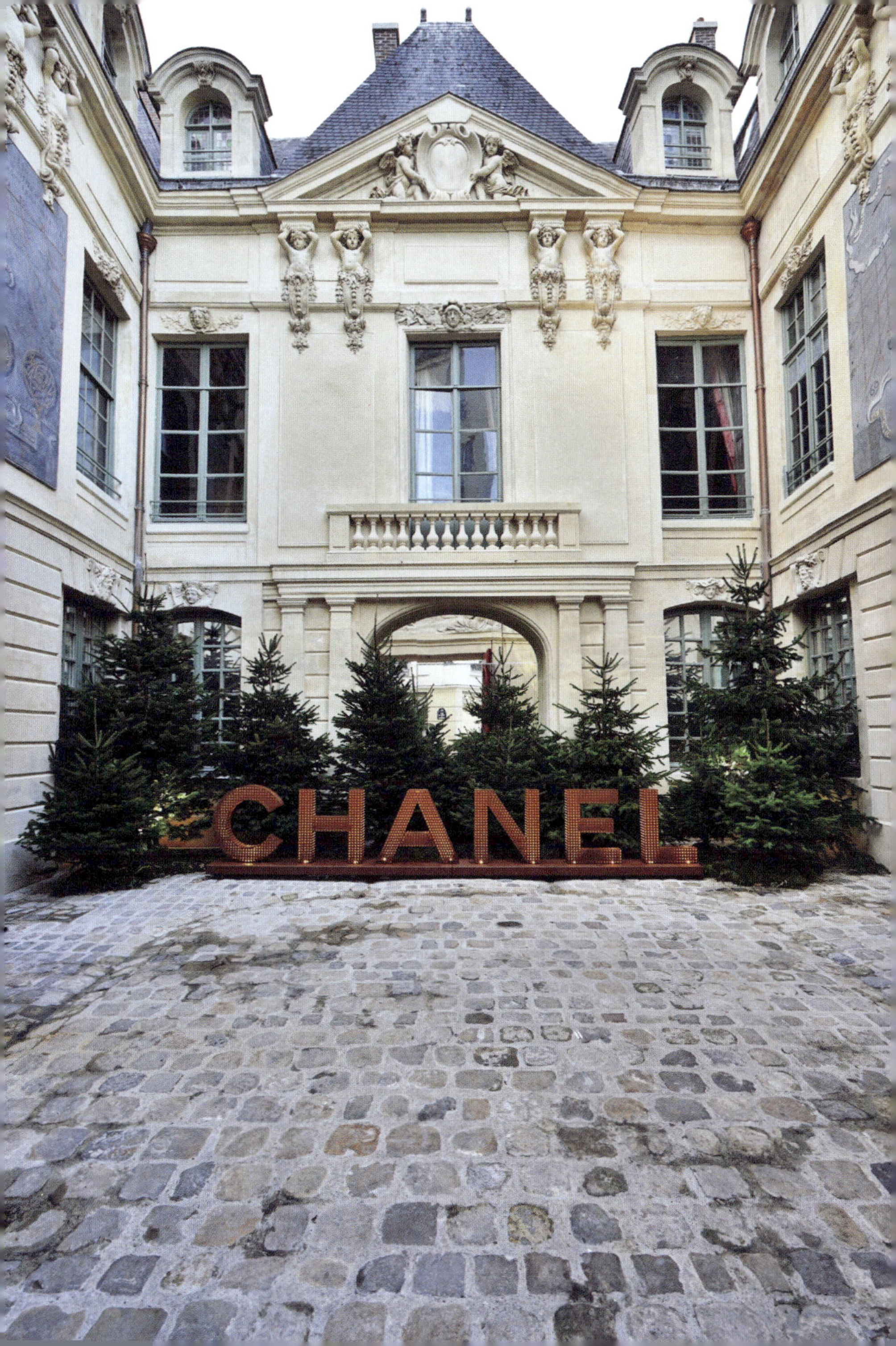
CHANEL

CREDITS

Helmin & Sorgenfri would like to thank the following for permission to use images in this book.

Album	Alamy Stock Photo	7
Heritage Image Partnership Ltd	Alamy StockPhoto	8
PictureLuxThe Hollywood Archive	Alamy Stock Photo	11
Sebastian423	Dreamstime.com	12
Wikimedia Commons		13
Album	Alamy Stock Photo	16
Fashionstock .com	Dreamstime.com	19
firstVIEW		20
Valentina Linnik		21
Abaca Press	Alamy Stock Photo	23
firstVIEW		24
COMEO	Shutterstock.com	27
firstVIEW		30
adsR	Alamy Stock Photo	31
Featureflash	Dreamstime.com	32
Valentina Linnik		34
mimilee	Shutterstock.com	35
RobertWei	Dreamstime.com	37
AS photo family	Shutterstock.com	38
Valentina Linnik		39
ZUMA Press, Inc.	Alamy Stock Photo	41
GRANGER Historical Picture Archive	Alamy Stock Photo	45
Nicoleta Raluca Tudor	Dreamstime.com	46
INTERFOTO	Alamy Stock Photo	47
FashionStock.com	Shutterstock.com	48/49
firstVIEW		50
Abaca Press	Alamy Stock Photo	51
firstVIEW		53
INTERFOTO	Alamy Stock Photo	54
Valentina Linnik		58
adsR	Alamy Stock Photo	59
Natalia Hanin	Dreamstime.com	60
Dmitry Morgan	Dreamstime.com	62
Studioportosabbia	Dreamstime.com	63
Suradeach Seatang	Dreamstime.com	63
Valentina Linnik		63
Dmitriy Melnikov	Dreamstime.com	64
Mykhailo Polenok	Dreamstime.com	65
Natalia Hanin	Dreamstime.com	67

IanDagnall Computing	Alamy Stock Photo	68
Anna Watson	Alamy Stock Photo	73
Valentina Linnik		74
Abaca Press	Alamy Stock Photo	75
Zhi Qi	Dreamstime.com	76
patralak	Shutterstock.com	77
firstVIEW		78
firstVIEW		80
WENN Rights Ltd	Alamy Stock Photo	81
Abaca Press	Alamy Stock Photo	82
Valentina Linnik		86
GRANGER - Historical Picture Archive	Alamy Stock Photo	87
PictureLuxThe Hollywood Archive	Alamy Stock Photo	88
Abaca Press	Alamy Stock Photo	91
Retro AdArchives	Alamy Stock Photo	92/93
Ttatty	Dreamstime.com	94
firstVIEW		97
MediaPunch Inc	Alamy Stock Photo	101
Abaca Press	Alamy Stock Photo	102
firstVIEW		103
firstVIEW		104
Grzegorz Czapski	Alamy Stock Photo	107
Abaca Press	Alamy Stock Photo	108
firstVIEW		109
firstVIEW		110
firstVIEW		111
Patti McConville	Alamy Stock Photo	113
firstVIEW		114
Anwar Hussein	Alamy Stock Photo	119
Anwar Hussein	Alamy Stock Photo	120
WENN Rights Ltd	Alamy Stock Photo	123
Tinseltown	Shutterstock.com	124
Tsuni USA	Alamy Stock Photo	125
Matteo Chinellato	Alamy Stock Photo	127
Featureflash Photo Agency	Shutterstock.com	128
Featureflash	Dreamstime.com	130
Starstock	Dreamstime.com	131
Fred Duval	Shutterstock.com	132
Abaca Press	Alamy Stock Photo	137
kovalenkovpetr - stock.	adobe.com	138
agcreativelab - stock.	adobe.com	138
EQRoy	Shutterstock.com	141